Gospel of the Stars

The Mystery of the Cycle of the Age

Born in 1936, **Peter Lemesurier** read languages at Cambridge and holds the Associate Diploma of the Royal College of Organists. He has been a musician, jet pilot, trimariner, teacher and translator. He is the author of many books whose subjects range from philosophy and psychology to the Greek Gods, prophecy and the Ancient Egyptian Mysteries.

By the same author

The Armageddon Script
Beyond All Belief
The Cosmic Eye
The Great Pyramid Decoded
The Great Pyramid: Your Personal Guide
The Healing of the Gods
This New Age Business

Gospel of the Stars

The Mystery of the Cycle of the Ages

PETER LEMESURIER

ELEMENT BOOKS

First published in 1977. This edition
first published in Great Britain in
1990 by Element Books Limited
Longmead, Shaftesbury, Dorset

Drawings by Pamela Jenkins
Diagrams by Ray Smith
Designed by Roger Lightfoot
Typeset by Selectmove Ltd, London
Printed and bound in Great Britain by
Billings Ltd, Hylton Road, Worcester
Cover design by Max Fairbrother

Front cover photograph: Aspect Picture Library

British Library Cataloguing in Publication Data
Lemesurier, Peter, *1936–*
Gospel of the stars: the mystery of the cycle of the ages
1. Signs of the zodiac
I. Title
133.52

ISBN 1-85230-148-1

Note
Throughout this book, the generic term 'man' and the associated
pronominal forms 'he', 'his' and 'him' are used purely for linguistic
convenience. In all such cases the words 'woman', 'she' and 'her' are
of course equally implied.

Contents

Foreword

The subject of this book is aeonic astrology. It is concerned with the vast cycles of the zodiacal ages and the seasons of the cosmos as they affect humanity at large. Consequently it makes no claim to explain the esoteric influence of your particular sun-sign or to give personal advice regarding your financial, emotional or medical life. Important such things may be, but even more important is the larger, universal context within which both occur.

I do not deny that you may have chosen to be born under a particular configuration of sun, moon and planets. If so it would not be too surprising if that configuration in turn, like the shape of your head or the lines on your palm, reflected to some extent your foreknowledge of your own fate.

I do not deny, either, that there may be unseen links between the movements of the heavens and the phenomena of the terrestrial sphere. The assumption, as we shall see, was certainly basic to the science of the ancient world, and it is reflected in our own day in the Jungian notion of synchronicity. In which case it would not be too surprising if your own fortunes were linked to the movements of the heavenly bodies, just as they apparently are to everything else.

Nor do I deny the possibility that those skilled in such things may be able to use their knowledge of the heavens to enable you to bring to the surface of consciousness your own deeper knowledge of yourself. Indeed, even many of those who are *un*skilled in such things seem able to use the stars much as a diviner might use tea-leaves, and to treat the celestial sphere as a kind of crystal ball – a device for occupying and mesmerising the conscious mind while its deeper counterpart probes and lays bare the secrets of the collective unconscious.

All these things are as may be. But it is perhaps worth remembering that the heavenly vault and the wheeling galaxies are not there to serve you or me. Rather are we here to serve the universe. And in particular the signs of the zodiac, we may be sure, were not devised to enable us to dabble in personal divination.

But note the word 'devised'. For the signs of the zodiac have no independent existence. The stars do not form patterns. Their distribution across the night-sky is quite random. There are no Twins, no Bull, no Ram, no Fishes, no Water-Carrier. It is we who create those patterns; we who then impose them on the stars. The pictures that we see in the upside-down teacup of the heavens are images of our own devising. It is humanity's own insights that are out there among the stars.

As we join up the dots of the celestial star-puzzle, interpret the ink-blots of the ultimate in Rorschach tests, what are revealed to us are the secrets not of outer but of inner space. The limitless inner space of our own consciousness. The unfathomable well of human vision and foreknowledge.

By looking outwards we see inwards.

And so, by contemplating the dance of the galaxies, the rhythms of the universe, we may start to gain new insights into man's real nature. For he is inevitably part of that universe. Its rhythms are his rhythms. Its cycles are his cycles. It is the very pendulum of the cosmic clock that makes man tick.

And it is with the dawning of that realisation that the ancient signs and symbols of the celestial zoo start to work their magic upon us. For those images are no more than our own deeper selves in disguise. We are the gods. We ourselves are the heavenly archetypes. Through the zodiacal signs and symbols we project ourselves upon the darkened screen of the night-sky, observe our changing rôle in the cosmic dance, learn to prepare ourselves, like growing children, for the greater dance, the Real world that lies beyond.

But if mankind as a whole has a larger destiny to fulfil, it is on the efforts of individual men and women that the eventual outcome must depend. What is true for man in general is also true for you and me. The pattern of the macrocosm is inevitably reflected in the microcosm.

Each one of us, in short, is a vital cog in the machine, a part of the greater universe. Willy-nilly we must reflect its rhythms or perish. And a condition of that reflectivity is that, in our meditation, we still the deep pools of our consciousness. Still them until they become a mirror, faithfully reflecting the celestial vault above . . .

Thus, gradually, the ancient vision may once more find its focus deep within us. Not only the vision of man's greater rôle in the essentially cyclic process of cosmic evolution, but, on a more homely level, that personal vision which can enable each one of us to 'place' himself psychically within that process and its periodicities, and so to understand the events of his own life and times in their true cosmic perspective.

From such an exercise we may all hope to gain a greater sense of purpose and proportion. From understanding the universal symphony as a whole each player may hope to achieve a better and more fulfilling performance, whether during the more discordant and chaotic passages of history or during the intervening moments of serenity and calm. Both, it soon becomes apparent, are essential to the over-all opus. Both, consequently, are of positive value, and demand our full co-operation.

On the personal level, too, the over-all view may cause our occasional failures to loom less large, our equally occasional successes to seem less important. And instead we may come to value the experience of simply Being Here Now, at this particular time and place, each doing what we have to do.

Part One

The Procession
of the Ages

For everything its season, and for every activity under
heaven its time:
a time to be born and a time to die;
a time to plant and a time to uproot;
a time to kill and a time to heal;
a time to pull down and a time to build up . . .
Whatever is has been already,
and whatever is to come has been already,
and God summons each event back in its turn.

Attributed to KING SOLOMON (Eccl. 3:1–3, 15)

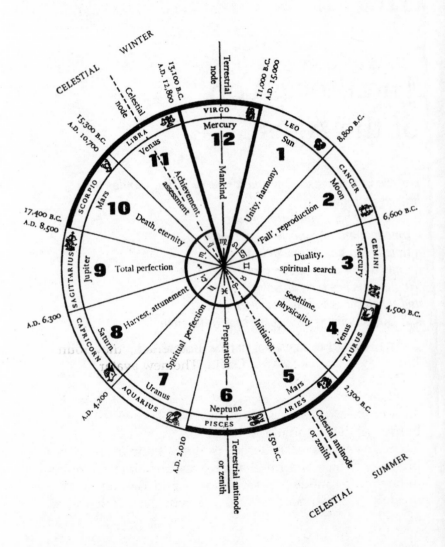

The Cosmic Clock, showing the months and seasons of the astrological Great Year.

1

The Mission of the Magi

I am Alpha and Omega,
the beginning and the end,
the first and the last.

Rev. 22:13 (A.V.)

Onward they journeyed, those three Wise Ones, in search of a miracle. Astrologers all, they had seen the rising of a star, the dawning of a new dispensation. Long they had journeyed to do homage to the new Messiah. The old wisdom must defer to the new. Soon they would present him with their strange, prophetic gifts, the symbols of his destiny. Gold for the king. Frankincense for the priest. Myrrh for the death and resurrection.

And there, in David's city of Bethlehem, they found him. The child. The star of David. The new avatar.

Or so we are told.[1]

What had they really seen, those three Wise Ones, in the ancient skies? What was the nature of their knowledge, the burden of their aspirations?

The answer, we shall see, is not a simple one. The premises which inform that answer are almost wholly unfamiliar to modern man. And to find the key to the mystery we shall need to look with new eyes at the place of man in the universe. Or rather with old eyes. For our task is nothing less than to rediscover man's ancient stance before the stars.

Nature, we know, is cyclic. The universe abhors straight lines no less than it does a vacuum. The days, the tides, the seasons, the moon's phases, life and death, the ecological cycle, the dance of the galaxies. Nature forever moves in cycles, and any theory – whether of biological evolution, social progress, cosmic creation or human spiritual destiny – which attempts to reduce that progress to a straight line graph does violence to the laws of nature. Nature is not like that. And we ignore the fact at our peril.

Man has evolved on a turning planet to a cosmic symphony of cyclic rhythms that is faithfully reflected even in the breathing of his lungs and the beating of his heart. So long as he remains man he cannot escape that periodicity. He is reborn to it from generation to generation, from age to age.

But if he is cyclic because his environment is cyclic, then there must surely be links between the two. And if his body reflects the rhythms of day and night, of the four seasons, of the turning years, should there not be similar links between the greater rhythms of the universe and the deeper movements of his very mind and soul? What of the eleven-year sunspot cycle, the nineteen-year solar eclipse cycle, the motions of the planets, the twenty-six thousand year cycle of the polar 'wobble' or precession of the equinoxes? What of the forty thousand year variation in the earth's angle of tilt, the ninety-two thousand year cycle of orbital eccentricity?

The science of the ancient world may not have been as objective or as self-advertising, nor certainly as materially successful as our own. Clearly it was less violent in its methods. Its aim was to understand the processes of nature in order that man, through his understanding of them, might learn to work with and through his environment, rather than thinking he has to struggle against it. Compared with our own science it was the soft approach – the water which, in the end, will wear away the hardest stone.

And like water it flowed everywhere, into every nook and cranny.

Not for the ancients our modern refusal to take into account what we cannot measure, our shutting of the eyes to anything beyond the purely physical. To them the human environment, the greater universe, was no less mental and spiritual than it was physical in nature, and if there were deeper links between man and the universe, between microcosm and macrocosm, then they too needed to be investigated. While the ancients were in no way as well equipped as we are to investigate man's physical environment, they were every bit as well qualified as we are to explore the realms of mind and spirit.[2] And the links, to them, were explicit.

A cyclic universe of cause and effect – this was the concept basic to the outlook of the ancient initiates, men such as the legendary Magi.[3] As above, so below.[4] On earth as it is in heaven.[98] Down here, suffering mankind struggling, not for the first time, slowly and painfully towards the light. Up there, the pulsating clock of the universe, reflecting and timing the evolutionary cycle of our planet.

And, for the Magi, a new hour had just struck.

Once every twenty-six thousand years, so the astronomers reveal, the slightly bulging waistline of the spinning earth causes it to complete one revolution of its polar wobble. And the angle of the planet's tilt is by no means constant, its orbit neither fixed nor circular. Consequently the angle of the sun's rays regularly changes, their intensity varies, the climate alters, sea-levels rise and fall.

Now the northern ice cap advances, whole species of fauna and flora are wiped out, man retreats to shiver in the caves or migrates to warmer climes. Now the ice withdraws northwards again, sea-levels rise by three hundred feet or more, whole lands are flooded, whole communities disappear, new civilisations and technologies are born.[5]

Rhythmically. In recurring cycles.

Rhythmically, too the full moon of harvest – immemorial herald of the ancient new year – appears to move backwards through the heavens at succeeding autumn equinoxes, backwards against the mighty stellar backdrop. Until it comes back to the point where it started. Once every twenty-six thousand years.[6]

Man, then, needed but to look up at the heavens to see the moving finger of his destiny. For above him hung the great cosmic clock in all its splendour. Not only the sun to rule the hours of the day, the constellations to mark the progress of the night, the lunar phases to control the months and seasons. But also the starry companions of the harvest moon to signal the tempers of the succeeding ages. By reading their silent auguries, man might hope to attune himself to the purposes of heaven. In cosmic harmony his life and work might then prosper and his destiny go forward to fulfilment.

To the ancients it was of course natural to see the harvest as the time of the old year's end and the beginning of the new. How should it be otherwise? The time of reaping and fruit-gathering would soon be past; the time of ploughing and sowing was about to begin. Now was the time when the coming year's fortunes would be decided. Decided as much by man's own response to nature as by nature herself – as mirrored in the stars. What was needed, therefore, was some unifying symbol, some celestial reference-point. And so, to the Wise Ones of the ancient agricultural communities, the ripened fruit of the moon's disc at the time of the festival of harvest became a moving finger that wrote amid the dust of the stars the destiny of the new year's seed.

But with the rise of the cities the Wise Ones too ceased to be country dwellers. The ploughing and sowing, the farmer's careful work and preparation, became lost to sight. It was only when the green shoots sprang up into the warmth of the spring sun that the resurrected life of the new year started to impinge on the general consciousness.

So it was that the vernal equinox in turn came to be celebrated as the time of new year. Easter, the festival of new life and resurrection. And instead of the harvest moon, it was the revivified sun that became the celestial symbol of the new beginning, the guardian of the year.

Yet it was all one. The Wise Ones were wiser than they seemed. They knew what the common man perhaps did not – that those same stars which clustered about the harvest moon also hovered, unseen, at the shoulder of the Easter sun. The self-same stars that ruled the ancient lunar year now ruled its solar counterpart. Terrestrial man may have altered his sights, but the celestial clock, unchanged, untiring, continued to reflect and record his destiny through the ages.

But it is not sufficient for the hands of a clock – be they sun or moon – to move across an unmarked face. If the symbols were to be read, the ancient lessons learnt and applied, the clock-face of the heavens must be reduced to order, divided into twelve distinct divisions after the model of the former lunar year.[7] And within those twelve divisions the constellations must be given names and identities – identities that would reflect the terrestrial developments that would accompany the sun's passage through them. So out of their deeper consciousness the ancients now projected symbolic images upon the uncaring and chaotic stellar canopy – a sort of cosmic Rorschach-test, a divination in reverse imposed upon the inverted teacup of the heavens. And out of it all came the twelve signs of the zodiac – the timekeepers of the polar wobble, the guardians of the equinoctial precession, the lords of the ages, the symbols of human destiny.

Nor was that all. For to each of the twelve divisions the ancients now assigned a ruler, to each heavenly kingdom a god, whose character and attributes might further reflect the burden of his age. In their classical form these gods assumed the guise of Mercury, Venus, Mars, Neptune, the tumultuous succession of Uranus,[75] Cronus (or Saturn) and Jupiter, and the solar and lunar deities.[8]

Onward they came then, in slow procession, those shining ones, as the heavens slowly wheeled, for each in turn must establish his rulership over Gaea, the earth. And, looking upwards, the ancient peoples thought to see those same gods in the 'wandering stars' – the heavenly shining ones which are our familiar planets, sun and moon, and which now bear their names.

Thus it was that, some four thousand years before the birth at Bethlehem, the position of the sun at the spring equinox had passed out of the sign of Gemini and into that of Taurus, while the symbolic sceptre passed from Mercury to Venus.[8] Two thousand years later, and the sun was passing from Taurus into Aries, thereby conferring rulership on Mars. And now, with the coming of the Magi, the age of Aries was likewise drawing to a close, as it laboured to give birth to the age of Pisces . . .

But what did these images really mean for man? What vital knowledge was it that the ancients wished to pass on via this ultimate in visual aids? What could the Magi have seen that was so earth-shaking in the passage of our solar star across a purely artificial division in the ancient heavens?

The answer, it seems, concerns the very nature, identity and destiny of man. And to unravel it we shall have to turn back that clock, unwinding the cycle until we come to the age of Libra.

It is not, of course, in the nature of a cycle to have a beginning or end, any more than nature itself has a beginning or end. Even the universe, suggest the Hindu scriptures, merely undergoes an unending cycle of explosion and implosion, as it bursts at intervals of some four thousand million years through the cosmic interface between matter and anti-matter, existence and non-existence.[9] But a cycle will normally have a low point and a high point, just as a wave-form has a node and an antinode.

And the obvious node of the zodiacal traversal, as its

very symbol suggests, is the age of Libra.

Libra is the point of balance, the fulcrum of the zodiac, straddling both old and new. Its corresponding dates on earth are 15,300 to 13,100 BC.[8] But earth requires time to take up the celestial rhythm, in the phases of terrestrial evolution no less than in the seasons of the year. There is a time-lag before life on earth can find its corresponding node. Libra's scales, alone among the signs of the zodiac, are a mere inanimate symbol standing for a mechanical cosmic process. It is a further two thousand years before they give way to a symbol that has life.

The *terrestrial* node falls exactly where one would expect – in the midst of Virgo.

The Constellation Virgo

Virgo is the Virgin. She represents both the starting-point of the human reproductive cycle and, as its final product, its end. In the Babylonian tradition she is 'the ear of corn' – the product, but also the seed, of the vegetation-cycle. In whatever terms, Virgo brings both the triumphant conclusion of one cycle and the promise of another. She is the Winter Solstice, the terrestrial link between old and new.

Why, then, assign her symbolism to an earthly age? What did the period from 13,100 to 11,000 BC have to do with archetypal virginity? Who, in short, was the virgin in question?

Perhaps the word 'earthly' is the key. For if the vision of the ancients concerned the nature and evolution of man, it concerned no less the evolution of Earth herself. The two were in no way separate. Man was the ultimate offspring of Earth, the child of his planet. And the planet, for its part, was the physical womb from which he had sprung. Gaea,[75] the Earth-Mother.

If, then, Gaea had now taken on a Virgan rôle, man himself could not be unaffected. His destiny and hers were intertwined. They must go forward in unity or not at all. The universe is One.

And so we may start to unwrap the mystery, to decode the ancients' vision. For a new cycle of earth's history was about to begin. Gaea had attained her womanhood. Her childhood was past. And now the Virgin herself had conceived and was with child.[10] Announced, it may be, by an archangel. *Archangelos*, the ruling messenger. Who else, then, but Mercury, *ruler* of Virgo,[8] *messenger* of Jupiter, herald of God the Father? Who else but Hermes, the divine magician? *Hr-ms*: Horus-is-born.

Hermes is more than elusive: he is quicksilver. At times of crisis and transition he appears as it were out of nowhere. Then he departs again. His function is to facilitate change, to bring the new to birth. His methods are secret, arcane, unexpected. He brings with him qualities of intelligence, originality, fleetness of foot and manual dexterity. He is a natural improviser, an opportunist through and through. Cunning, even deceitful, he will take what he needs without the slightest scruple.

He is a born survivor.

Thus it is that the cunning of Hermes promises an autonomous magic, a new beginning, a transformation. His advent in the world at large heralds a reborn humanity. Hence his appearance as Mercury in the age of Virgo, the Archangel's annunciation to the Virgin.

For there in the depths of remote antiquity a miracle was about to take place. Kissed and embraced by the Divine, the Earth-Mother was about to give birth. A god had come to dwell in her midst.[11] A new generation of humanity was conceived, a new order initiated. It was time for human souls to take up anew the ancient adventure of terrestrial experience.

So, at least, the symbols would suggest. But do we read them aright? What does our knowledge of the earth's remote past tell us of the age of Virgo? Does it in any way confirm our interpretation?

Because if it does, then it may be that we have indeed discovered part of the key to the mystery.

Consider the world-map. Nearly all of the earth's land-mass lies in the northern hemisphere. The far south, apart from Antarctica, is almost wholly ocean. So, when the planet's slow gyrations beget an ice-age, almost no new southern land is swallowed up by ice. Nor is much of the earth's water locked up in it, for most of it returns to the salt ocean, which never freezes far below its surface.

But the northern ice cap does spread. And when it does, vast stretches of North America, Northern Europe and Siberia disappear beneath the ice. Its frozen water cannot return to the ocean. Sea levels fall. New lands appear at the edges of the continental shelf. And man must either stand and fight, or flee the approaching winter and set up home in these 'new lands'.

Until the northern thaw at last returns.

As return it did – along with the historical age of Virgo. For this was the age when the fingers of the northern ice last began to loosen their ancient grip. Reluctantly

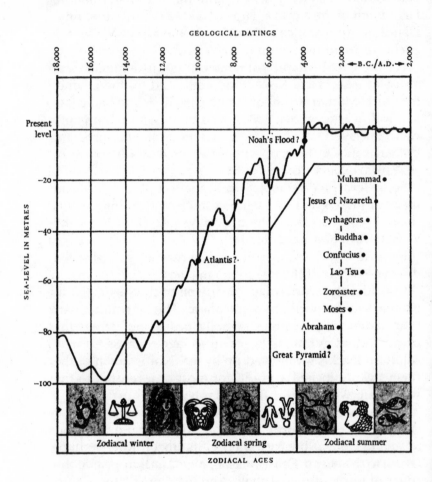

GEOLOGICAL DATINGS

THE ZODIAC AND THE TERRESTRIAL ICE-CYCLE
as reflected in world sea-level changes (lowest levels reflect maximum glaciation). Based on graph from Rhodes W. Fairbridge, 'The Changing Level of the Ocean' (Scientific American, May 1960, Vol. 202, No. 5).

and spasmodically at first. Then ever more surely. And soon, with world sea levels everywhere gradually rising, old lands, old cultures started to be drowned one by one. We do not need Plato's account of the legendary Atlantis to remind us of the fact.[12]

Yet out of this watery womb would come new life. Out of the death of winter would come a new spring. As the ice cap retreated, the vast plains of the northern hemisphere would start to be freed little by little for human habitation, new cultures could arise, and a new wave of human evolution would be generated by the need to travel, to tame, to innovate. Travel, animal husbandry, innovation: three provinces that are sacred specifically to Hermes. As the old world of Virgo neared its end, the new world of Leo held the promise of a great rebirth.

The symbols of the ancients and the facts of history are one.

Meanwhile, mythologically, the age of Virgo should have been the era, above all, of the sacred mother-goddess and the midwinter cult of virgin and child. But then the notion has never been fully absent from the human psyche. It was present in nearly all the later vegetation-cults of the ancient Middle East – whether Babylonian, Persian, Egyptian or Greek – and it was therefore already an extremely well-worn and familiar hand-me-down when it was eventually inherited by the child of Bethlehem.

With Virgo, it seems, we have found the key to the ancients' code. Now we can turn it. Little by little, perhaps, we can open the door to the heavenly mansion and decode the rest of the zodiacal revelation.

In 11,000 BC we enter the first of the celestial rooms. Its guardian is Leo, its ruler the sun itself. And *its* message at least is clear.

For with the age of Leo the sun indeed comes out. The first age of the new cycle has begun. It is the world's springtime. The tawny Lion's face, set in a halo of flaming

The Constellation Leo

hair, is the image of the blazing solar disc. And as the sun begins to smile on the vast, new, spreading heartlands, man can once more feel at one with nature, at one with himself.

The unity and wholeness of this obviously Golden Age is reflected in its symbols. For not only is Leo, like all the zodiacal signs, a direct function of the solar precession. His ruler is the sun itself.[13] The sun, in short, is in its own house, master in its own kingdom. And the sun, throughout the zodiacal progression, symbolises nothing less than the soul of man, as it passes from stage to stage of its evolutionary way, *en route* for a greater destiny.

Leonine humanity, then, is a being at peace, at one with itself, in an age of psychic wholeness. We see that age's monumental archetype in the great Egyptian Sphinx at Giza (whose real age may yet surprise us). The Lion's animal body, the lord of nature in balance and repose, is surmounted by an erect human head, the symbol of man's alert higher faculties. The higher man in harmony with the lower. *Mens sana in corpore sano.*

And the gaze of the Sphinx – long revered as Harmakhis, solar lord of the horizon – rests firmly on the equinoctial sunrise.

And so, mythologically, this is the age of the sun-cult and its mysterious standing stones, symbols of the descending solar rays. It is the first age of the Egyptian zodiac.[14] Now that man is once more surrounded by burgeoning life, he can observe its response to the solar cycle. In symbol, he attunes himself physically to its rhythm, steals the sacred fire from heaven. Observing and celebrating the solstices and equinoxes, he makes of his whole life a solar festival, honouring the earthly fire no less than the heavenly.

The cult of the sun, meanwhile, is that of Helios/Apollo. In both incarnations it is knowledge that is the prime element. Sheer intellectual savvy and know-how. In the earlier case of Helios it is a knowledge that can sometimes get in the way of practical achievement, a proneness to over-confidence and accident. In the later case of Apollo the lessons have been learnt. Knowledge is tempered by wisdom, know-how by moderation. 'Man, know thyself' is merely 'Nothing in excess' in other words. Know your limitations.

And so the foundations are laid for later civilisations. The regularities of the heavens are translated into the rules and regulations of an ordered society. Through the Titan Prometheus the heavenly fire is brought down to earth for the material benefit of humanity. In however primitive a form, science, mathematics, craftsmanship, architecture stir into action. So does the technology of the chase, and particularly the skill of archery. For Apollonian man is tough; Promethean humanity still resilient. Pitting himself against the elements and the creatures of the wild, the child of Leo fashions for himself an ideal world of his own devising. A veritable golden age ensues.

That age will of course not last. Every sun must move towards its setting. The inner demands of Apollo are great, and not to be satisfied without a price. The triumph of the head presupposes the devaluing of the heart. In time the emotions will be disregarded, intuitions scorned. As order supplants chaos, and 'rational' man comes to lord it over 'irrational' woman, aggression, egotism, paranoia, power-mania will be given their chance. Cracks and divisions will start to appear in the world-wide social fabric. Man will become sundered from woman, man from man, family from family, tribe from tribe, people from people. And ultimately humanity from itself.

But only because the sun-cult in its turn was to survive far beyond its cosmic time. In Persia, in Egypt, in Rome, no less than in the megalithic sun-cults of the far Atlantic seaboard, it persisted until at least the time of Christ. Even the Messianic Essenes of first-century Palestine took the sunrise for a symbol of rebirth and future glory.[15] And the bearing of the summer sunrise from the archetypal Sphinx, the guardian of the Giza necropolis, still leads from the pyramids of its three kings (whose polar passage-angles that bearing faithfully reflects) to the city of Bethlehem.[16] (See opposite)

With the passing of the age of Leo and the birth of Cancer in 8,800 BC, the great northern thaw had already been in full swing for some millennia. True, the old lands were still being swallowed up by the rising waters, but their area was as nothing compared with the vast northern tracts that had now emerged from under the ice into the sunlight.

Nature, after a brief setback, was bursting into life as never before in human memory. For man there was a whole new world in which to live and move and have his being. There was space. There was freedom. And now that the land could support him, he could afford to breed.

And that is the message of Cancer. We commemorate the fact even in the language of modern medicine. Cancer is the sign of reproduction, of unbridled growth for good or ill. The spreading of man's wings.

Cancer is the Crab, a creature whose appearance is a function of the tide and thus of the moon, of the sea and

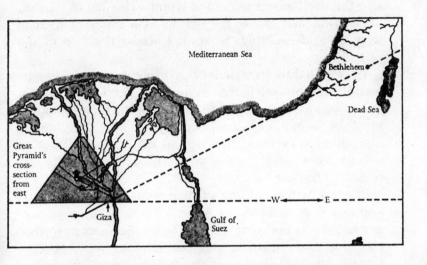

The rhumb-line bearing of Bethlehem from Giza is identical to the Great Pyramid's main passage-angle – an angle common to the pyramids of all three 'kings' of the Giza necropolis. The line of this bearing also marks out the probable sites of the biblical crossings of both 'Red' Sea and Jordan. Furthermore, it defines (for the third millennium BC) the bearing of sunrise of 6th June and 7th July (assuming that sunrise is defined as the moment when the sun's disc is tangential to the horizon) – thus 'missing' the ancient midsummer sunrise itself by only 1.7°.

In this and other respects the Great Pyramid's messianic symbolism is intensely solar in nature, and this fact, plus the obviously Leonine symbolism of the Great Sphinx, guardian of the sacred places, might suggest for the original Pyramid a much earlier date than is generally assumed.

Meanwhile the building's brilliant outer casing soon earned for it the title **The Light (Ta Khut)** among the Egyptians, and cast star-shaped reflections on the desert around it. In all of which we may discern the makings of a persistent legend concerning three ancient 'kings' who were led by a 'star' – whether solar or otherwise – to the birthplace of a new Messiah.

thus all life. And the lunar rhythm, the tidal month, is also the rhythm of the human womb. The age of Cancer, the second age of the new cycle, is a time for man to increase and multiply, to spread across the face of the earth.[17]

The moon thus offers herself as the new symbol whereby man attunes himself to the cosmic process.[202] Its silver light announces a Silver Age. And the cult of the moon-goddess must be a cult of sexual fertility, linking the human reproductive cycle to the annual death and rebirth of nature itself, and thus also to the annual death and rebirth of the sun.

But not at the bidding of man himself. For the lunar goddess is pre-eminently Artemis/Diana. Dark and dangerous, she is her own woman, self-willed and powerful. Her moods are unpredictable, her motives unfathomable. Continually subject to warring emotions and deep, unconscious urges, she alone knows the seasons of her sexuality. When her time is ripe, she will co-operate passionately with those men who are continually drawn to her. But those who approach her at the wrong moment she will just as happily discard, emasculate, destroy.

And so Artemis represents the reverse side of the coin of her twin brother Apollo's intellectualism. To his head she opposes her heart. To his chauvinistic sexual manipulation she opposes a woman's will to self-determination. In the process she may, out of sheer reaction, turn into an Amazon, an out-and-out feminist. Sexually ambivalent like her brother, she may exhibit lesbian tendencies. Or, as the shy and retiring Selene, she may avoid human sexual contact altogether, preferring the company of horses. And all the while the occult techniques and arcane schemings of her *alter ego* Hecate, hag-like goddess of witches, beckon almost irresistibly out of the darkness. For with them they bring the prospect of summoning up all the powers of the unconscious to oppose and finally defeat the dominant Apollonian conscious mind.

The Constellation Cancer

Yet Artemis has a kinder, more creative side, too. She has green fingers. She is highly skilled with animals and young children. And as a mother her ferocity in protecting her own knows no bounds.

In the lunar age of Cancer, then, the mother-goddess, the religion of the sun, the lunar cult, the myth of the vegetation-god – all become mingled into a violent, ecstatic celebration of human sexuality synchronised with the seasons and the four great solar festivals. The solar standing-stone becomes a phallus. The physical is king.

And in the process, as those ancient draughtsmen of the zodiac foresaw, man starts to lose sight of his spirituality.[18] Unlike the leonine Sphinx, the Crab has no head. Or if he has, he hides it. In its place, only a pair of pincers. The left and the right – the physical and the spiritual. And both are used merely to feed and defend his body. As though in shame, he scuttles away, buries himself in the mud. Here, if anywhere, is the symbolic Fall.

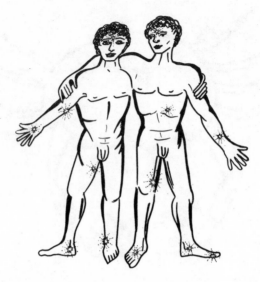

The Constellation Gemini

And consequent upon it is the mission of Gemini.

Gemini are the Heavenly Twins, the archetypal brothers whose legend survives into later ages as that of Castor and Pollux, of the Aztec Gagavitz and Zactecauh, of the kings of Atlantis,[19] of the biblical Moses and Aaron. Aaron is the human mouthpiece, Moses the god he speaks for.[20] Likewise Castor is the suffering mortal, Pollux his immortal counterpart. Yet Pollux, archetypal *bodhisattva*[21] that he is, will not, cannot, claim his immortality until Castor has achieved it too. Moses cannot reach the Promised Land until the people of Aaron, the enlightened bearers of *aron* (the ark), have fulfilled their task.[22]

Man, in short, is subject to psychic schizophrenia. He has a foot in two worlds, an eye to two realities. And he cannot achieve his true destiny until he has learnt to reconcile and re-unite the two.

Man must first awake to this psychic duality, and then

realise that it is no more than unity in disguise. He must become aware that the spiritual and the physical, the inner and the outer, the above and the below, are but two serpents entwined about a single staff, which is the staff of his power and his destiny. But let him forget either of them, and his destiny must remain unfulfilled.

This was the message of the later Moses, when he fashioned a single brazen serpent on a stick to be a talisman against snake-bite – a warning to a people who had their eyes fixed firmly on the physical instead of the spiritual, on the ground instead of the stars.[23]

And so the symbol of Gemini is the doubly snake-entwined wand of Mercury, herald of Jupiter and winged messenger of the gods, who reminds man that there are two sides to his nature and to his destiny. Mercury is also Hermes, or Thoth, the god of healing, whose eventual task is to reunite the two halves of man's nature and make him whole. And both gods are, of course, no more than man's own higher nature in disguise.

And so, as the wandering Hermes returns once more, a new crossroads is reached. The time has come to take a new road, to undergo a further initiation. But this time its theme must be paradox. The paradox of the shaman or medicine-man who must go mad to preserve the tribe's sanity, playing the fool in pursuit of deeper wisdom. The paradox of the wounded healer who is also a perfect charlatan. The paradox of the sage who abandons everything to discover that he lacks nothing. The paradox, indeed, of the Dioscuri, Castor and Pollux themselves, the idealistic and mutually self-sacrificial boon-companions who are at the same time the crassest of professional muggers and bandits.

Paradox, the heart of the riddle, the core of the parable.

Mercury's alter ego, as we saw earlier, is quicksilver; his age, it seems, a continuation of the Silver Age of Cancer. In this guise his function is to silver the mirror of human consciousness, to hold up to man the reversed image of himself that is his soul. Thou art that.[175] The notion is purely Geminian. The age of Gemini, in short, is an age for reflection, for introspection.

Know thyself.

Man must look into his real nature and rediscover his soul. He must decide which of him is image, and which is reality. Then the fire must separate from the stone.[24] The forgotten spirit must take wing. It is the third age, the age for spiritual exploration, an era for hermetic initiation into the mysteries of the secret god, its figurehead the Thrice-Great Hermes, Trismegistus. The Inner and the Outer Wisdoms must grow, first separately, then together, until with their final synthesis in a future Jupiterian age they engender a great new step in human evolution. Cupid and Psyche, *ruach* and *nephesh*, immortal and mortal are reunited. And man, stepping through the cosmic mirror, at last becomes whole again.

Bear in mind, meanwhile, that it is for the returning Prodigal Son, and not for his brother who never left the Heavenly Mansion in the first place, that the fatted calf of Taurus will eventually be slain.[25] The Geminian Fall of man, it seems, far from being his undoing, is the essential precondition for his ultimate glory.

Of the age of Gemini and its mythology scattered traces still remain. For its chief cult, inevitably, was that of the serpent. And so to this day tradition speaks of the ancient serpent-power as the guardian of all wisdom. In North America it left traces among the early Mound-Builders; in Central America it gave rise to the legend of Quetzalcoatl, the Feathered Serpent; in China to the cult of the Dragon; in India to the *kundalini* concept. In Egypt the serpent served both as a sign of Osirian initiation – the *uræus* or 'restored eye of Horus' – and as a symbolic boat whereby the Pharaoh might gain the shores of immortality. Its myth looms no less large in the ancient traditions of both Greeks and Hebrews, where it often lurked as a thing to be feared, as though the symbol of some ancient and forgotten trauma deep within the collective unconscious. Yet to

Jesus of Nazareth (as to the earlier Moses) its overtones were less sinister: he felt able to advise his followers, for instance, to be as wise as serpents and as innocent as doves.[26] But then both men had Egyptian connections, and may have been privy to the Egyptians' ancient lore.

Meanwhile some would have it that the web of the former serpent-power still criss-crosses our planet today, in the 'power-grid' of 'ley-lines' and 'power-points' which has long been the subject of so much speculation.

Speculation, necessarily, because they belong to an unknown age. An age of which we have no written records. The last of such ages. The age before the dawn.

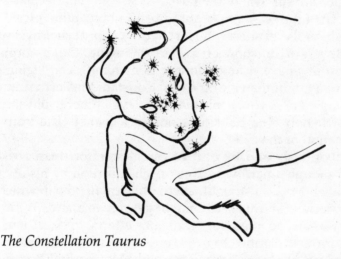

The Constellation Taurus

For with the coming of Taurus we reach the frontier of recorded history. It is with his glyph   that the most ancient alphabets will eventually begin. The date is 4,500 BC. In the sacred fruits of Venus,[8] in the apple newly revealed by the Geminian serpent and duly proferred by Eve, man (=Adam) has rediscovered the source of self-knowledge, the seed of his being. Now he must plant it. That, in short, is the message of the Bull, the story of Eden.

As at the later Nineveh, Taurus was once a winged bull. But now it had lost the power of flight. Lucifer/Venus, the morning star, had fallen. No longer could Taurus graze the celestial prairies. Instead it had become the lowly, earthbound ox, a beast of burden and a plougher of the soil. For this was the fourth age, the earth-age, the age for agriculture.[27]

It is not hard to read the symbolism. The theme of the moment is fertility. The fertility of Aphrodite, the irresistible sex-goddess who lures men on, releasing their inhibitions through light-hearted play and humour, and thereby contrives to assure the much more serious business of the survival of the race.

Born of the sea-foam, Aphrodite is bubbly, effervescent. But she is also evanescent. Her charms cannot last. Physical fertility is a function of a mere moment. Other forms of fertility have a much longer-term remit. The lifelong creativity of human life on earth. Constant intellectual and aesthetic endeavour, spiritual self-development, physical construction. The transformation of a planet. The transformation of the race.

Laboriously and by dint of ceaseless effort man must now plough a narrow furrow of self-salvation by his own sweat and toil – a straight, even, physical furrow in which the precious spiritual seed might germinate anew.

It was an age, then, for prodigious efforts, for Herculean toil, for self-sacrifice to a hitherto unheard-of degree. In the physical sphere no less than in the spiritual. The soul redeemed by sheer physical effort. The path of *karma-yoga*. The age of the megalith. The age of the pyramid.[28] And ever urging him on, his own higher nature found a new use for the staff that had become in turn the solar standing-stone, the Cancerian phallus and the wand of Mercury. Stripped now of its twin serpents, it had become a goad, a prodding-stick, a ceaseless reminder to wavering man that he had a destiny to fulfil.

And so the chief cult of the age of Taurus was indeed the bull-cult. The cult of El, Semitic bull-god and prototype of

Allah, the cult that was to survive into later Minos and Egypt, Babylon and Assyria, Greece and Rome. The cult that still survives today in secular form in the Iberian peninsula. Man must first tame, then sacrifice the bull of his own physicality, for it was the blood and vigour of that bull that alone could give life to the growing seed.

Mithras, *alter ego* of the living sun, must first master, then slay the cosmic Bull. And attuning himself to the myth, man was to make of it a sacred symbol for the redemption of his soul.

It was easy, none the less, for ignorant man to confuse appearance with reality. It was natural for the popular mind to assume that there really *was* a bull-god grazing somewhere out there among the prairies of the galaxies. A god who would somehow redeem mankind, as though by proxy, without any real effort on his own part. A scapegoat. A saviour. And it was even easier for the later priesthood to pander to the superstition. For even priests are men, and just as lazy.

And it was no less natural that the same fate should befall the symbol of the next great zodiacal age. For hard on the heels of Taurus came Aries. The Ram.

2300 BC. The symbolic corn had sprouted. So, too, had the lush green pastures, the grasslands of the spirit. Man's next cosmic task was plain. He must feed. Feed on the truth that was growing in his soul. He need have no other worries, no other cares. The sheep may safely graze. The flocks must grow strong. For there were testing times ahead.

The groundwork had been done, the soil dug. There were no more lands to conquer. No longer did man need constant prodding from behind. All that was needed was a kindly shepherd, one who would guard him and prevent his straying from the flock. One who would lead him to fresh pastures as the need arose. Man must become a nomad on the grasslands of the spirit.

This, then, was an age for great prophets and priest-kings to arise, the shepherds of the people. The fifth age, the age of the initiates. An age for following the instructed ones through whom the spirit would lead the people. Even to Bethlehem.

And so this must be the era of the cult of the Ram. The Egyptians would institute the cult of Amun; the Israelites, that of the Passover lamb.[29] And the former goad of man's higher nature must be transformed into a shepherd's crook – no longer an instrument of positive encouragement, but a means of negative restraint. Man must bridle his lower nature in order that his soul might grow. The plant must be cut back in order that its leading-shoot might be strengthened and bear fruit. Witness the apparent negativity of the Mosaic Ten Commandments[30] and of the teachings of the Buddha. For he, no less than Moses, was aware of the Signs of his times, and attuned to the spirit of his age.

In ancient Greece, too, the Arian tradition of discipline would duly set in. It was to be the age of classicism. The ancient gods, with their swashbuckling romanticism, were progressively banished to the world of fairy tales, and in their place the philosophers installed a succession of abstract principles to which all things must be seen as being subjected. For Pythagoras it was number, for Anaxagoras mind; for Heraclitus (no less than for the Chinese authors of the *I Ching*) it was eternal change. The humanistic Sophists cut back the plant even further, remodelling reality in the image of man's own thought. Until, trimming and modifying the ensuing systems of Socrates and Plato, Aristotle the classifier applied the final blinkers to the consciousness of Western man, and set him firmly on the analytical and, in practice, materialistic track which he is still following even today.

Yet myths are not so easily banished. The gods will not go away. In all of this the Greek philosophers were still unconsciously deferring to the dominant myth of their age – the spirit of Aries. And it was in response to that same spirit that Jason must now set out in his *Argo* – the celestial *ark* or solar boat that bears the avatar of each new age – in symbolic quest of the Golden Ram's Fleece, the mighty totem held by Aeetes, son of the sun. But in order to seize that fleece, that Arian reflector of the divine solar glory – for such it was – he must first challenge its former guardians, the never-sleeping serpent and the fire-breathing bulls. He must wrest the destiny of Arian man, in other words, from the powers of Gemini and Taurus.

Meanwhile, when the migrating Israelites revert to the worship of the Bull, Moses angrily destroys their golden calf.[31] The cosmic symbols must serve only their due season. The fulfilment of man's destiny depends upon his attunement to the cosmic process. The microcosm must reflect the macrocosm. Only in harmony can the Plan go forward.

In Moses, then, we see a manifestation of the Arian initiate. He is a combination of shepherd and warlord. For his heavenly guide is Jehovah, lord of hosts, captain of armies, just as the celestial ruler of Aries is Mars, god of war.

The Roman/Mars is the Greek Ares. And indeed the nature of Ares fits the case perfectly. Churlish and brutal when crossed, self-willed, belligerent and if need be vengeful, he nevertheless tends to mature with time. And as he does so his other qualities come to the fore. His military genius. His taste for organisation and control. His penchant for idealistic self-sacrifice.

And so Mars/Ares is the spirit of the dictator, the lawgiver, the wreaker of vengeance. His regime is patriarchal, typified by the imposition of rules and restraints. And rightly so, in the context of the age of the Ram. The Arian avatar must first repress in order that he may liberate.

But if the ram was to be the sacrificial beast of the new dispensation, the talisman of the human soul, what of the physical function of the ancient bull? In so far as there was still a physical task for man to perform in pursuance of his

The Constellation Aries, with Triangulum (possibly the secret sign of the Ass)

destiny, what was to be its sacred symbol? The bull, after all, had served not only as sacrifice but as symbolic beast of burden. How could the poor ram do likewise?

In any other society the question might not have arisen. The ages were blurred, often indistinguishable. The sacred symbols – all of them functions of a single sun, a single Higher Nature – could be interchanged, could last beyond their time. Earth-Mother, sun, secret god and sacred bull continued to exert their spell throughout history: the crab-cult of growth is still with us today. But in Palestine the age of the Bull was dead and past. If there was to be a symbolic beast of burden, then it must be the ram – or some substitute animal. An animal, moreover, which was sacred to no other zodiacal age.

But which animal?

The answer lies half-hidden among the ancient writings and traditions. An answer known only, it may be, to the ancient Masters and initiates. But there, unmistakably, it was.

The donkey.

It was the Ass whose name was henceforth to be coupled with the former Ox. It was the Ass whose dark and volcanic cult now arose in Egypt as that of Set or Typhon (whose sign was Y) to complement that of the Ram (compare the Aries sign   ). And it was the same Ass, the same Set/Typhon, who was to serve as war-god to the Semitic Hyksos, while their Hebrew cousins preferred to be led into battle by their god Jehovah, lord of the martial cult of the Ram. Yet even among the Israelites, the Mosaic dispensation of Aries was to be inaugurated at Mount Horeb amid a Typhonian paroxysm of volcanic fury.

Set/Typhon, lord of the volcano, was, it seems, the dark alternative, the dreaded *alter ego* of the Arian Divinity, the *yin* to the *yang* of Jehovah. Which might explain why, in Egypt, Set was always seen as the negative, or 'dark aspect' of his brother Horus. And why, in later years, there were to be persistent rumours of a secret ass-cult in the temple at Jerusalem.[32] In the night-sky, too, the same occult tradition was perhaps reflected. For in the inverted triangle of the constellation Triangulum (compare the sign Y) the Ass, it seems, may have lurked anonymously in the shadow of the celestial Ram, calmly awaiting its share of the limelight.[33]

And so it is no surprise when the Hebrew prophet Zechariah has the Piscean avatar enter his kingdom upon the back of a donkey, dreaded co-symbol of the former age. The kingdom of heaven must descend on earth,[98] prevail over the forces of darkness. 'On a foal,' he insists, careless of practicalities, 'the young of a she-ass'.[34] The Hebrew words themselves suggest a clue to the nature of the mystery. For it is *ayir*, the Ass's colt, that must now stand proxy for *ayil*, the Ram. The sacred tongue itself seems to have had a hand in the symbolic process.[35]

And it was in around 150 BC that the age of Aries finally came to a close.

Thus it is not only appropriate, but almost a symbolic necessity, that the eventual prophet and symbol of the new age, the Piscean avatar, should be born in a stable. For both Ox and Ass must now be seen to bow before him. The legendary shepherds, too, must forsake their zodiacal sheep of the Arian dispensation and hurry to embrace the symbol of the new.[36] The child of Bethlehem.

And hard on their heels, the three Wise Ones (or was it the Thrice-Great, Trismegistus himself?).

Through all the stations of the zodiac, from Virgin through Lion, Crab, Twins, Bull and Ram, they had followed the star of the new-born child in its royal progress down the halls of human history. *For the sun was his star*. The Light of the World.[37] The Dayspring from on High.[38] Ever since the great cycle began it had led man, through a myriad settings and risings, from the promise of planetary renewal, via his fall into physicality, to the new birth of the spirit.

And now it had led him to Bethlehem.

So, bearing the wisdom of yesterday, the Magi prepared to meet the truth of tomorrow. The old must defer to the new. The eternal pilgrimage.

Bowing under the low doorway, they went in. The great star stood directly over the house.[39] It was noon. The cycle had reached its zenith. The sixth age had begun.

2

The Cosmic Fisherman

Come with me, and I will make you fishers of men.
JESUS OF NAZARETH (Matt. 4:19)

The Constellation Pisces

The young Galilean who came down that day to the Jordan for baptism[40] was no stranger to the practice. Like the preacher who was his cousin he knew that it was a daily ritual throughout the Essene monasteries of desert Palestine.[41] It was both purification and ritual rebirth. Drowned in the uterine waters of the symbolic womb – the womb of the Earth-Mother – the postulant emerged into the sunlight to begin his life anew. From untruth to truth. From darkness to light. From death to immortality.[42]

Such was the nature of baptism. A ritual for the raising of the drowned.

Who, then, were they, those poor drowned souls? Who were the symbolic dead who needed to be raised to life? Who were the denizens of the lower darkness, the uterine waters, the waters of mortality?

Who else but the fishes?

Consider the symbols. The waters themselves are a fixed symbol throughout the Hebrew scriptures. A symbol for death, for imperfection, for mortality. The Flood is a reward for wickedness and a bringer of death; and only those ark-borne souls who, with Noah, rise above it can reach the post-diluvian world, the land of the living.[43] Later the Red Sea in turn becomes a pit of death for the Egyptians, and only those who can cross it dry-shod live, with Moses, to reach the other side.[44] The Jordan, too, must be crossed dry-shod if the followers of Joshua are to enter the Promised Land.[45]

The Land of the Living, the Other Side, the Promised Land. Ciphers, one and all, for immortality, for eternity. Only by rising above the waters of mortality can immortality be gained. Only by leaving the waters of the womb can the child of man be born. The notion is no more than logical.

A logic reflected in the symbol of baptism.

And swimming to and fro in the waters of mortality are the fishes. The fishes of Pisces. The astrological fishes who are, by tradition, bound together. Fishes who are therefore prisoners of each other, and so also of the uterine waters they swim in. Karmic prisoners of mortality, bound by their own umbilical cord, awaiting their birth and freedom.

We are those fishes.

We are those prisoners.

We are the unborn dead.

Who then will raise us to life? Who will be our midwife?

Consider our predicament. We, the fishes, the flocks of the sea, are masters of our watery element. We can move in it at will in any direction. Unlike the sheep of Aries we can move not only horizontally, but also in the vertical. Even to the very interface with the world above, the limit of our consciousness. Yet beyond that limit we dare not go. Perhaps we do not fully believe in that higher world. And even if we do, we merely people it with our own reflections in the tantalizing mirror that undulates uncertainly above our heads.

But if we do not understand that higher world, we fishes comprehend our own world little better. We feel water, drink water, breathe water. To a large extent we *are* water. Unable to conceive of a world without it, we therefore take that water for granted, cease to be aware of it. We cease to believe in the sea.

To put it in plain words, we are surrounded and controlled by mortality. We are mortals. But because we are unwilling to admit that ultimately, in whatever terms, we are dead, we cannot see the necessity of being raised to Life.[46]

And yet see it we must. For out there lies the next step in our evolution, the goal of our gestation. Out there, whence come the light, and thus the oxygen, without which even this watery existence would be impossible. Life must move out of the sea and on to the dry land. It is a fixed decree of the universe, reflected in the zodiac itself. How, then, shall we be persuaded to move with it? How shall the child be induced to leave the womb?

And that is where we come to the rôle of the fisherman.

For the spirit, incarnating as the Christos, is the fisherman of the Piscean age. Like a dove it descended on Jesus at his baptism[47] – the returning dove of the Noah-story,[48] the homing pigeon of the reincarnating Christos. Like a dove it raised him from the waters as the new-born avatar. But that was a swift process of the spirit, a rushing mighty wind, a voice from heaven. For most of mankind more patience would be necessary. The slow patience of the angler. The dangling hook.

Baited with bread.

Bread made from the corn that had been planted in the age of Taurus and had sprung up during the age of Aries. The spiritual corn, the corn of the initiates, that had ripened with the zodiacal summer and had at last been harvested.

The bread of Bethlehem.[49]

It was the daily or 'supersubstantial' bread requested in the Lord's Prayer,[50] the bread of the miracle of the loaves and fishes,[51] the bread of the Last Supper that was to be a new symbol for salvation.[52] The crumbs from the Master's table which even the gentile dogs might eat.[53]

The bread, too, which, dipped in the fatal bowl, was to be the signal for the Master's own self-sacrifice.[54] And take note of the symbols. The bread dipped in the bowl is the bait cast into the waters – the bread of enlightenment. Judas is the fish who takes it, swallows the hook. One result is physical death. The other is spiritual salvation.

That is the message of the Piscean age. At all costs the fishes must be caught.

But there are two fishes in the sign of Pisces. Two fishes that are bound together. Two linked directions. Two complementary possibilities. Man, it seems, must now explore both his higher and his lower nature, his light and his dark aspects. He must learn to recognise and accept his irrational as well as his rational side, his unconscious promptings no less than his conscious reasoning. But then he must make a deliberate choice. For within their watery prison the fishes of Pisces are freer than the sheep of Aries. Free to rise or to descend. Free to take the celestial bait or to reject it. Each must find its own level. Choose thou.

Nevertheless on that decision will depend each man's destiny. On that decision will depend whether he leaves the lower world behind and rises to a new plane of existence – or whether he remains in the watery darkness of the womb and shuns the world of light. Either decision involves a death, whether of the upper or the lower nature. But the one decision accords with the direction of cosmic evolution. The other goes against it.

Yet remaining is more comfortable: leaving is an effort. Consequently the fishes decline to bite. The catch is poor. The child declines to be born.

And so the cosmic fisherman which is man's own higher nature resorts to sterner tactics. The angler of the Christos lays aside his rod and line and takes up his fish-spear. He becomes Neptune with his trident, waiting to spear the choicest fishes.[8]

Yet in reality it is still the fishes who do the choosing. They can swim within range of the trident, or they can stay well clear. And once again, most prefer to stay well clear. Like Hamlet they would rather bear the ills they have than fly to others that they know not of. Such is the nature of man. And fish.

But Neptune is also the Greek Poseidon, and Poseidon will not be thwarted. He is not only the beneficent ruling deity of spring and stream, but the mighty god of tidal wave and earthquake. That earthquake may be an outer, physical one or an inner, psychic one. But when the time is ripe Poseidon is quite prepared to shake his victims to the roots, to turn their world upside down, to shatter everything that they hold most dear, to lay all their achievements in ruins. Arising out of the dark waters of the unconscious, he will overwhelm the puny structures of their conscious will and leave behind nothing more than a featureless sea of virgin mud to serve as the basis for a new dispensation entirely.

And so a new initiative is called for. *Retiarius*, the gladiator with the trident, closes for the last time with *murmillo*,[55] his fish-helmeted quarry. And now he must deploy his ultimate weapon.

The net.

With the end of the Piscean age a great, fine-meshed net must be let down into the sea.[56] The very chasms of the ocean must be dragged. Every fish must be dredged up for assessment. Every human soul must come up for judgement. Even at the risk that those from the blackest midnight depths may burst apart in the process.

But judgement for what? What becomes of the fishes that are caught?

How does the fisherman normally react? Those that are too small he returns to the sea. They need more time to grow, to fatten, to develop. Many are called, but few are chosen.[57] Those that are big enough he keeps. To eat or to preserve. In the case of the Piscean fisherman, he keeps them alive – in a fish-tank, a pail, a pitcher. That pitcher, with its precious contents, he must then pass on to his successor.

For his successor is the mighty Aquarius.

Meanwhile it was Jesus of Nazareth who had taken on the rôle of cosmic fisherman, the avatar of the Piscean age whose symbol was the fishes. The *bound* fishes. And so it was in these terms that his life was lived and his teachings constantly couched. Even from his baptism.

For a start he joined the fishermen.[58]

Who they really were and where they had come from is anybody's guess. It may or may not be significant that the Essene scribe of Qumran, source of the Dead Sea Scrolls, wrote at about this time: 'Thou hast caused me to dwell with the many fishers who spread a net upon the face of the waters, and with the hunters of the children of iniquity.'[59] Certainly the imagery, already beloved of the priests of Isis, was apt to the Piscean dispensation. Certainly, too, the Essenes were no strangers to zodiacal lore, as surviving documentary fragments reveal.[60]

The Essenes' overriding preoccupation was atonement – the idea that the new birth of the human spirit, the expected Golden Age, could somehow be forcibly induced by the deliberate act of a 'righteous remnant' of the people. They themselves, they believed, were those self-same righteous ones. It was their own total commitment and purity that would qualify them to act as midwives to the new birth. But, curiously enough, the Hebrew for 'righteous one' (*tsaddiq*) is related to the verb *tsadah* (to lie in wait) – and thus to *tsade*, the Hebrew for fish-hook. So once again we come back to the rôle of the fisherman of the age of Pisces. The title was as applicable to the Essenes as it was to Jesus and his followers.

'Come with me, and I will make you fishers of men,' called Jesus to the Galilean fishermen.[61] And both he and they knew perfectly well what he meant.

We need not doubt, then, that the parable of the loaves and fishes relates to the self-same theme. For parable it almost certainly was in the first place. A parable of the coming Messianic Banquet, the Golden Age, the Kingdom of Heaven on earth. Its subsequent editing into two different episodes of supposed history we may safely ascribe to later embellishment and the religious zeal of the evangelists.[62]

The story's theme is the rôle of the Son of Man, the Messiah of Jewish expectation, the Piscean avatar – or perhaps his Aquarian successor. How, it is asked, will he satisfy the needs of his followers? How will the shepherd that is man's higher nature feed the sheep of the former dispensation? The answer comes in symbolic form. The five thousand he will feed with five loaves and two fishes, the four thousand with some fishes and seven loaves. In the first case twelve baskets of fragments will be left over, in the second, seven.

The numbers are significant. Five is the traditional number of initiation, four that of the earthly or physical. Seven stands for spiritual perfection, while two is the dynamic number of reproduction or manifestation. Twelve is a firm symbol for mankind itself – the twelve tribes of Israel, the twelve apostles, the twelve signs of the zodiac which reveal man's destiny. The bread is the bread of enlightenment, the 'supersubstantial' bread of the Lord's Prayer. And the fishes, it is quite evident, are fishes that have already been caught – caught with that self-same bread. They are the saved, the initiates.

And so the riddle is solved. The initiates (the five thousand) will receive further initiation and enlightenment (five loaves) at the hands of the great Enlightened Ones (two fishes – the respective avatars, or manifestations, of the Piscean and Aquarian dispensations). Their acquired enlightenment must then be put to the service of mankind as a whole (there must be twelve baskets of fragments). Having themselves become fully enlightened, these same initiates (the indeterminate fishes of the second version) will have the job of rescuing their own more earthbound brethren (the four thousand) through the spiritual perfection of their own enlightenment (seven loaves). The result will be an age of spiritual perfection (seven baskets of fragments). And the association between the baskets of both versions and the pitcher of Aquarius might suggest that this latter development indeed belongs to the seventh, or Aquarian age.

The initiated disciples, in short, must become the midwives of the new birth. From the caught fishes of one age they must become the fishermen of the next. The fishers of men. Set a thief to catch a thief.

But first, find your fishes.

So the work commences. And gradually the catch grows. More and more fishes are hooked with the bread of Piscean enlightenment. They are the elect, the self-chosen, the one hundred and forty-four thousand, the men of men (12×12).[63] The basket starts to fill. Soon there are signs of life in the heavenly pitcher.

The idea spreads. One of the caught fish, the Pharisee Paul, founds the Christian church. Soon it is distributing its own bread, making its own converts, conferring its own initiation. The leaven of the Pharisees.[64] The mere crumbs from the Master's table, the mere fragments remaining from the miracle of the loaves and fishes, become the bait for the fishes of the gentiles.

And meanwhile the ancient symbols are faithfully preserved, dutifully reflected in the new and spreading cult. Its members are initiated through ritual immersion, the drowning and rebirth of Piscean baptism. Emerging from the waters, they are given a secret sign, the historical symbol of the early Christian brotherhood, the sign of the fish. Now they are placed in the charge of an overseer. A bishop. In the Greek which was their common tongue he is *episkopos*. It cannot have escaped their notice that the word itself contains the Latin root meaning 'fish' (*pisc-*), or that the word as a whole could even be construed in Latin as referring to *the work of selecting the fishes*. And the overseer is duly arrayed in the symbols of the Christian dispensation, the dispensation whose task is to bring the sheep of the age of Aries into the Piscean fold, to substitute the New Covenant for the Old, the path of light for the ways of darkness.

Yet the new still has its roots in the old. Its rôle is to complete, not to destroy.[65] And so, as the bishop brings the newly-caught fishes into the nave which is the ship (*navis*) of the church, he is still given the shepherd's crook of Aries to lean on, symbol of the age of the Old Testament. But on his head is placed the crown of the New, the mitre, in the shape of a fish. The caught fish whose open mouth gapes ever skyward, in the direction of eternity.

Meanwhile Jesus too has taken ship.

Through calm and storm, in good weather and in foul, by night and by day he directs and supervises the work of the Piscean fishermen. Men who have already made the great leap from death to Life.[66] Children of the new birth. Strangers in the world. Aquarians before their time.

When the storms blow up, he calms their fears. Even the waves seem less steep.[67] When the catch is poor, he locates new shoals of fish – the fish to whose welfare the whole age is dedicated.[68] And they are caught on the right, or 'spiritual' side of the boat.[69] When the weather is calm, he guides the masses on the shore.[70] In symbol they are the Arian sheep who have not yet dared to enter even the baptismal water of the Piscean dispensation.

Triumphant over the waters of death, he encourages

his foremost disciple, too, to walk on the water, to place mortality under his feet. And when Peter sinks in the attempt he raises him again from the watery element, the kingdom of the fishes and the drowned.[71]

Already in the age of Pisces, in short, Jesus takes on the rôle of the future Aquarius. As the prophecies repeatedly require, he is to set the prisoners free.[72] The cosmic midwife. The pourer out of the water of the womb. The rescuer of the fishes. Already he looks forward to the age that must follow.

For the Piscean age is the sixth age. The age of preparation. Its avatar must therefore himself become a prophet, the forerunner of the seventh.

The herald of the sabbath.[73]

3

He That Should Come

Destroy this temple, and in three days I will raise it again.

JESUS OF NAZARETH (Jn.2:19)

The Constellation Aquarius with Piscis Australis

Jesus had good reason to be at the marriage-feast at Cana in Galilee, scene of the changing of the water into wine.[74] For the Son of Man was himself the bridegroom. The bridegroom of the parable from which the story originally grew.

We may reconstruct that parable.

The wedding guests have arrived. Already they are drunk. Drunk with the wine of the old dispensation. Already the wine has run out. The six stone pitchers, the cisterns of the sixth age, stand empty. The old dispensation is dead.

Where, then, is the bridegroom? Still he does not come. The hostess goes in search of him, the mother seeks the son. In symbol the chosen virgin, the Earth-Mother, offers her womb to the child. For Gaea must give birth to Uranus,[8] who must in turn become her heavenly bridegroom.[75] The fire must arise from earth and then return to transform it.[24] The Messianic conception.

The message comes back. He will come in his good time. And his time is not yet.

But that time is coming, and then the heavenly bridegroom will swing into action. First he will cause the six pitchers to be filled with water. Then that same water, the lifeblood of the age of Pisces, will be poured out. Poured out in the tradition of Aquarius. And behold, a miracle. For the water will have turned into wine. The new wine of the Aquarian age, of the Millennium, of the Kingdom of Heaven on earth. Now at last the long-awaited Messianic Banquet can begin. The cosmic wedding-feast. The marriage of man to his soul.[76]

Not for the last time the Nazarene had uttered a solemn parable. A parable of the end of Piscean time. A prophecy of the dawn of the age of Aquarius.

Again and again his words and his acts look forward to that great event. For the Aquarian age, he knew full well, was to be not only the crown of his own age but the culmination of those that had gone before. It was the seventh age, the cosmic sabbath. And on it, as he himself taught, the ox and the sheep (or ass) might be rescued from their well;[77] the fallen souls of Taurus and Aries might finally escape from their pit of darkness. The uterine waters of Piscean mortality would at last become a well of life.[78]

It was to be an age of rebirth, no less. In Hebrew

parlance it was called the 'Reborn World'.[79] And unless man were born again he could not see that Kingdom of Heaven.[80] For the two things went together. Willy-nilly, the earth would bring those long dead to birth again.[81] In more senses than one.

Hence Jesus' long explanation of the process to the Pharisee Nicodemus.[82] Hence, too, his insistence that man must become a little child if he would enter the Kingdom of Heaven.[83] For he must come again to birth, must become a new-born babe in the Kingdom of the spirit.

The child of Aquarius.

But the birth was destined to be a difficult one. For the god of the coming age, the ruler of the new heavens, was Uranus, the son of Gaea. (Even the biblical Kingdom of Heaven was always, in Greek, the kingdom of *ouranos*.) Serene and beneficent that ancient sky-god might once have been in the days of his youth, the very embodiment of light and grace, of fecundity and spirituality. But his patriarchal benevolence was already turning to violence and domestic tyranny. Male chauvinism was rampant. And so, as he brandished his new-found powers,[84] flexed his cosmic muscles, she, the Earth-Mother, would suffer violent convulsions. The planet would be sent reeling by disturbances in deep space. There would be planetary collisions – a comet, or worse. Earthquakes would follow. Volcanic dust would hood the moon and turn the sun to blood. Famine and pestilence would stalk the lands. Wars would rage. The very survival of life on earth would be threatened.[85] Such would be the birthpangs of the new age,[86] the advent of the long-awaited sky-kingdom.

And then, in the aftermath of the twilight of the gods, the promised new dawn. The coming of the Son of Man.
The birth of Aquarius
It would be as in the time of Noah.[87] The coming avatar would be one who had risen above the great flood, the tide of evil that had laid waste the earth. In the celestial ark of enlightenment – the solar boat of the pharaohs –

the spirit of the age had been biding its time, awaiting the end of the age of darkness, the re-emergence of the land from the uterine waters, the stranding of the Piscean fishes. And now, as the age neared its end, the world would see the coming of the Aquarian emissaries, the expected Messiahs. Noah sends out his shore-sighting birds.[88]

The first is a raven. A scavenger. One who seeks out the stranded fishes from among the debris of destruction. He flies to and fro with his catch. A rescuer. A messenger. For the fishes of Pisces are to be the harvest of Aquarius.

Now the dove, the Holy Spirit, descends.[89] At first it finds nowhere to roost. The second avatar is still unwelcome. The Son of Man has nowhere to lay his head.[90] The ancient flood has not yet fully receded.

But the third avatar, the dove of peace, finds a more ready response. The earth offers up an olive-branch. A gesture of peace, of reconciliation. A reciprocal gesture. The betrothal of man to his long-lost soul.

And so the dove of the spirit descends for the last time. And this time the flood has finally dried up. The age of darkness and mortality is past. The spiritual seed planted in the age of Taurus, the mustard seed that had sprouted in the age of Aries, has at last grown into a mighty tree, the tree of the Kingdom, the Tree of Life. Now at last the birds can come and roost among its branches.[91] The doves. The incarnations of the spirit. The Aquarian avatars.

The celestial Noah can disembark. Noah, whose name means 'rest', can descend upon the earth. The Aquarian cosmic sabbath can begin.

But what is to be the sign of the coming of Aquarius? What else but a sign written in the stars, a heavenly sign? A brilliant light which, say the scriptures, will arise in the east and spread as far as the west.[92] *Even the sun.* The precessional sun of the spring equinox, passing on its way out of Pisces and entering the gates of Aquarius.

The sign of the prophet Jonah.

For Jonah is the biblical fish-man, just as Aquarius himself was the fish-man of the ancient Babylonians. Jonah it is who is reborn from the Piscean belly of the great fish, who is restored to the land of the living after three days of darkness, who is cast up at last on the immortal shore, the Reborn World of Aquarius.[93] That the soul might rise to Life, the spirit must descend to earth. Jonah's sign, said Jesus, is to be the sole sign of the new age.[94]

And Jonah, in Hebrew, means 'dove'.

That dove returns, that spiritual pigeon comes home to roost, on the third day. The same 'third day' on which the Nazarene, too, promised to return.[95] The Hebrew phrase means 'the day-after-tomorrow' – 'in two days' time', as we reckon it. But in that case how long is a 'day'? If the Messianic 'day' is traditionally a thousand years,[96] then 'on the third day' means 'during the third millennium' – or after some two thousand years. Two thousand years after the laying to rest in the tomb that is the belly of the Earth-Mother.

An age must pass. A zodiacal age. Until, with the dawning of the third millennium, Aquarius shall emerge from the womb. And with him, mankind.

For Aquarius is man's own spirit. The celestial Son of Man who comes in the clouds of heaven with great glory. With a blast of the trumpet he sends out his angels, his messengers.[97] Lifting his great pitcher he pours out the glittering fishes. The caught fishes who are the returning initiates, the already-enlightened ones, destined to lead their fellows to the Light.

As in the heavens, so on earth the Kingdom has come.[98]

And so it was that Jesus of Nazareth embarked upon his last and royal progress to Jerusalem and death, making of it a symbol for the procession of the ages.[99]

'Go to the village opposite,' he told his disciples, 'and just as you enter, you will find a colt which no one has yet ridden.' *Ayir*, the foal of an ass. 'Untie it and bring it here,' he went on, and, anticipating a challenge, 'If anyone asks, "Why are you doing that?" say, "Its owner needs it."'[100] The owner of the lowly beast of burden which stood proxy for the Ram. The conqueror of Aries. The Piscean avatar.

The plan was deliberate, the symbolism no less so. The founder of the new age, the incarnation of the Piscean dispensation, must now announce himself as the Jews' promised Messiah by deliberately fulfilling the Messianic prophecies;[101] he must also proclaim his cosmic identity, his zodiacal rôle in the evolution of human consciousness.

Thus it was that his symbolic advent as ruler of the new age must be made upon the foal of an ass.[102] An ass that had been loosed from its captivity. A young colt that had never before been ridden. The sight would inevitably be incongruous – the full-grown man astride the diminutive donkey. A sign of humility, one might think. But at this point the approaching Piscean avatar, the anointed one of David, the royal Messiah, the predestined world-ruler or ruler of the age, had no cause for humility. *That* he would subsequently demonstrate in abundance. Now was his hour of glory. And in it he must above all respect the symbols of his office. The ruler of the Piscean age must enter his kingdom upon the symbolic back of his predecessor.[103] And so the necessary arrangements must be made, the beast held ready. And in due course its master claimed it, in fulfilment of the prophecies.

'Save us now, son of David!' chanted the excited crowds along the route, as they strewed garments and palm leaves in his path. '*Hosanna ben David!*'[104] Or could it have been *ben davvag*, 'son of the fisherman'?

And so Jesus finally reaches the temple and briefly goes in.[105] He returns on the morrow, and again on the following day.[106] Until the third day the Piscean avatar is in the house, teaching and instructing, casting his bread on the uterine waters. Until the third millennium the Piscean writ must run in the world and the Piscean enlightenment be given time to spread. The gospel of

Jesus must be preached throughout the planet.[107] But then the old order must fall and the new must take its place.

And so now, with the rôle of Pisces duly adumbrated, Jesus must go on to symbolise the coming dispensation of Aquarius.

'You see these great buildings?' asks Jesus as he leaves the symbolic temple for the last time. 'Not one stone will be left upon another; all will be thrown down.'[108] 'Destroy this temple,' he is elsewhere quoted as saying, 'and in three days I will raise it again.'[109]

The temple, the world-house, the whole dispensation of Pisces must be brought crashing to the ground, in order that the city of Aquarius may arise from the ruins. It will be of no avail to sew new patches on the old garment. The old wineskins will be unable to hold the new wine of the Messianic Banquet.[110] The old king must die in order that the new king may succeed to the throne.

The old king must die.

And it was to this climatic event that Jesus now turned his attention. To the death of Pisces which alone could make possible the resurrection of Aquarius.

'As soon as you set foot in the city,' Jesus was explaining to his two emissaries, 'a man will meet you carrying a jar of water. Follow him into the house that he enters and give this message to the householder: "The Master says, 'Where is the room in which I may eat the Passover with my disciples?'" He will show you a large room upstairs all set out: make the preparations there.'[111]

Jesus now had turned his attention to the great Passover festival which was to seal his cosmic mission. The Passover, symbol of salvation from the death of the firstborn. The Passover, symbol of escape from Egypt to the Promised Land.[29] From untruth to truth. From darkness to Light. From death to immortality.[42]

For the Passover-sabbath was approaching.[112] The seventh day. The day of spiritual perfection, when the great task of re-creating man would have been accomplished. The day of rest.[113]

In both Passover and sabbath there is already a clear symbolism. Both stand for a new age, a new dawn, a rebirth. Both hold promise of release, of Life, of immortality. Both celebrate the coming of the seventh age, the future age of Aquarius.

And now the symbols are made explicit. As soon as they set foot in that heavenly city, that new dispensation, the seekers who are the pilgrims of humanity will be met by a man carrying a pitcher of water. Not the woman whose normal task it was. But a man. A man who thereby identifies himself.

As Aquarius.

And as the celestial water-carrier comes to meet them, they in turn must follow him. To an upper room. A large upper room, already prepared.

'I go to prepare a place for you,' said Jesus. 'And if I go and prepare a place for you, I shall come again and receive you to myself, so that where I am you may be also.'[114]

And now, in symbol, that moment had come.

For there, in that large upper room which represents the limitless higher planes, the exalted dimensions of the coming Millennium, a feast had been prepared. The Passover-supper, the Messianic Banquet which throughout the prophecies had never ceased to symbolise the future Golden Age.[76]

And there in due course assemble the disciples, the faithful, the caught fishes of the Piscean age, for a ritual celebration of the ancient Passover-meal. A ritual with many of the characteristics of the Jewish marriage-ceremony, in the course of which the bridegroom washes the feet of the bride.[115]

And so Jesus, too, washes the feet of his disciples.[116] The Christos marrying itself to mankind. The reunion of man with his soul. The cosmic communion. 'If I do not wash you,' says Jesus, 'you are not in fellowship with me.'[117] Not married. Not one. The consummation of man's evolutionary struggle depends upon the washing of his feet by the Christos who is the heavenly bridegroom. The earthly Gaea must submit to the celestial Uranus.[75] And so Jesus, taking a pitcher, duly pours out the water into a basin.

And thereby identifies himself with Aquarius, the heavenly marriage with the Aquarian age.

And so the ancient ritual proceeds, and at its heart the eucharistic sharing of bread and wine.[118] The unleavened bread of penitence, the heavenly food, is the Piscean bread of enlightenment. But the wine, the poured-out blood, foreshadows the Messianic Banquet, the age of Aquarius, the Uranic conquest of Gaea,[75] the Kingdom of Heaven on earth.

On the one hand the old covenant, on the other the new.[119]

Foreseeing the dawn of that future age, the thirteen have become one.[120] In its golden light man has once more entered into union with his soul.

Meanwhile the time had come for the Piscean king to die.

The price of that death was thirty pieces of silver.[121] Coins such as that taken from the legendary fish's mouth, the first fish that came to the hook.[122] The fish that was Jesus. The money duly paid back into the temple that was the temple of the world.

Out of his own mouth he stood condemned, for the currency of his words spelt the doom of his age. The former world claimed its due. And he gave it. Yet now the Piscean temple could not hold the money. It must be re-invested, as the price of a new dispensation.[121] The old wineskins could not hold the new wine. The blood must be poured out.

And so the fish is duly hooked, the Piscean avatar is triply impaled. The trident of Neptune has found its mark. The catch is complete. Cross-borne, the serpent of Moses is hoisted anew.[123] Stripped naked, the secret god is revealed. Divested of its fleshly garment, the soul regains its immortality. And the spirit of the Son of Man is duly committed into the hands of the Heavenly Father,[124] the first-fruits of the fishes delivered into the pitcher of Aquarius.

It is the end of the sixth day, symbolic of the end of the sixth age. The Piscean task is done.

It is finished.[125]

Yet the world goes on, the cycle of the ages must continue. Let the body be pierced anew, let the celestial fisherman strike but once more, and blood and water will gush forth. For the master of the spear of Longinus,[126] the wielder of the spear of Odin,[127] is the Aquarian avatar. When, at his decree, the veil of the temple, the cosmic uterine membrane, is rent in twain,[128] the life-bearing water will be released and the Aquarian birth must commence.

And so, in anticipation of that future age, the body, embalmed with myrrh and aloes, is laid to rest in the tomb.[129] The sepulchral chamber that is both pitcher and egg. The womb of the Earth-Mother. From it new life is destined to burst forth in glory in the light of a future dawn.

The king is dead. Long live the king.

Thus our own Piscean age duly unrolls towards its appointed end. But what does it hold for mankind? In Jesus' recorded acts and parables we may find an answer.

In Mark's account we find such an answer in the story of the crossing of the lake, the Sea of Galilee.[130] And already we may suspect an allegory. For Galilee in the gospels is a symbol for the homeland, the land of the final return. 'I will go on before you into Galilee,'[131] promises Jesus, already seeing beyond his death, beyond his own time. Galilee stands for the coming Kingdom, the era of Aquarius. And as Jesus fully realised, his Kingdom was not of his age.[132]

And so when Jesus and the fishermen cross the lake to the other shore and then return to Galilee, we are faced with a set of familiar symbols. The souls of the first initiates, crossing the waters of mortality, will indeed reach the other shore, whence they will return only with the dawn of the New Age. To paraphrase Jesus, they will not again taste mortality until they see the Son of Man coming into his Kingdom.[133]

Other mariners embark as well. And in due course the leader falls asleep. In symbol, he departs from the world, leaving his remaining followers to carry on his work as best they can. But soon a storm blows up. The faithful are threatened. Eventually they call upon their leader to return to consciousness. Earnestly they beseech him to come to their rescue. In response to their entreaties he does so, calming their fears and restoring the world to rights. Like Moses, the Messiah returns as soon as the faithful truly desire it.[134] A righteous remnant suffices.[135] Such, it seems, is to be the advent of the Aquarian avatar.

Between the time of the Messiah's departure and his return as the new king, then, a time of troubles must come – a time which the faithful might be hard-pressed to survive. Well might they pray to be spared the test.[98]

The same impression is conveyed by a story from Matthew,[136] following directly on the story of the 'feeding of the five thousand' – a story which itself stands as an allegory of the mission of the initiates. This time the Messiah sends his disciples across the sea alone, while he himself withdraws to a hilltop to pray. In symbol they are the same followers as before, battling their way across the waters of mortality. But this time the disappearance of their leader is differently symbolised. It is the summit of the mountain that stands for the discarnate world, the land of the spirit.

Now the self-same storm blows up, and the night closes in. Those who have spent a wild night far out at sea in an open boat will know the feeling of hopelessness and desolation. But between three and six in the morning the

Master comes to them, walking on the sea. It is dawn. The Messiah is triumphant over the waters of mortality. The night is past.

Now the leading disciple, Peter, attempts the same feat. Walking on the water, he goes to meet the Master. He sinks, but is rescued by the approaching Messiah. And as soon as the latter steps into the boat, the wind drops. There is a sudden calm. Thereupon the boat reaches the shore, and all who come near are cured of their sickness.

Once again, the symbols speak of a turbulent age of darkness. An age when the faithful will be deprived of their leader. But deprived of his physical presence only. Spiritually it would be otherwise. 'Be assured,' he was to tell them, 'I am with you always, even to the end of the age.'[137] And it was then, at the end of the age, that he would return to rescue them in their hour of need. Even as his expectant followers set out to prepare for his coming they would be threatened with disaster. But in that self-same moment he would re-appear, raising them to new heights of glory. The world itself would be set to rights, and mankind would at last be made whole.

Let the faithful survive the age of darkness, then, and their salvation stood assured. A small remnant would suffice. *But they must survive*. For there would be wars and famines and earthquakes. False Messiahs would lead them astray. Men would turn against each other, betray each other. Lawlessness would spread. Love would grow cold. Life itself would come near to extinction. The whole planet would reel as vast cosmic forces were unleashed. That day would truly dawn in fire.[85]

Nor was the Nazarene alone in his view. The Hindus, too, had long foreseen the fate of the Pisceans. Piety would decrease, depravity spread. Property, wealth and lust would be the new gods. Appearance would lord it over reality, dishonesty over truth, menace over reason. Power would be all. And only when planetary cataclysm threatened would 'a portion of that divine being who exists' descend upon earth in order that the human psyche might once more become as pellucid as crystal, and man be born anew.[138]

And it is in this same context, the context of the end of the age, that we find the symbols of the earlier stories employed for the third time at the end of the gospel of John.[139] Again the scene is the Sea of Galilee. But this time Jesus has long been dead. We are here in the presence of a sacred allegory, a ritual and idyllic celebration, it seems, of the end of time itself. The end of Piscean time. The scene described for us is surrealist, dreamlike, almost magical.

Once again the fishermen are out on the water. This time they have spent all night fishing. They have caught next to nothing. But in the light of dawn the returned Messiah appears on the shore. 'Shoot the net to starboard,' he calls. To the right, or 'spiritual' side. And lo! on the right hand side of the boat the net is suddenly full of fishes – so full that it has to be dragged to the shore.

Again we may interpret the ancient symbols.

With the appearance of the Messiah at the end of the Piscean age the long night is over. The great net of the end of the age is let down into the sea.[140] Thereupon the waters of mortality yield up the harvest of a lifetime. And the great catch, the harvest of the spirit, is duly hauled towards the immortal shore, the threshold of the new age.

Now Peter, the foremost disciple, becomes impatient. 'The Rock' *puts on his tunic* and swims ahead of the boat some two hundred cubits to the shore. A strange detail – the opposite of what one might have expected – yet the symbolism is familiar. As in the story of the Garden of Eden, the garment which is put on is nothing less than the flesh itself. For in their primal state, Adam and Eve are 'naked' – that is, both immortal and discarnate. Their fashioning of clothes coincides with their assumption of mortality – and the symbolism is specifically that of the fig-tree, which stands for the physical.

And so Peter, in the story, clearly represents the former initiates who, seeing the approach of the Messiah, the coming of the Son of Man into his Kingdom, duly put on the garment of the flesh once more and 'go to meet' their Master at the end of the age. Reflecting the same symbolism, the world-representing rock of the Messianic Great Pyramid is clothed again to its full dimensions. Two hundred cubits stretch from its entrance to the south wall of its King's Chamber, the 'Chamber of Resurrection'. It is the distance to the shore of salvation, the distance to the Mystery of the Open Tomb.[16]

Mankind has arrived. There are one hundred and fifty-three fishes. And the number 153, in the New Testament world no less than in the Pyramid, is a firm cipher for the enlightened.[16]

There on the shore of eternity the Messiah is waiting. The Great Initiate is at breakfast. All night long he has fasted. Throughout the two thousand years of the Piscean age he has not tasted the fruit of the vine.[141] Now he has returned with all the power of the heavenly ones, the splendour of the celestial archetypes.

He is Hermes. He is Mercury with his wand. He is the herdsman who drives the Bull. He is the good shepherd. He is Neptune, the cosmic fisherman; Poseidon, the earth-shaker. He is the living Aquarius. He is the eternal Christ.

And there on the shore the bread of the new enlightenment is set out ready to eat. The newly-caught fishes are laid on the fire. The purifying fire in which the new age must dawn.[85] They are an offering, a sacrifice to the risen sun. The food which even Aquarius must pass on to his successor,[8] sacred to an age as yet unborn.

The dream hovers, becomes translucent. The former world dissolves into memory, a scarce-remembered song of long ago. The smoke rises into the sunlight. It is time to eat.

The Millennium has come.

4

The Age of Aquarius

I will pour out my spirit on all mankind.
                    The Prophet JOEL (2:28)

The age of Aquarius is almost upon us. AD 2010 is said to
be the official deadline.[142] But the precessional movement
is slow, the edges of the ages somewhat blurred. The
constellations are far from evenly spread about the ecliptic.
Some of them overlap. The imposition on the night-sky
of twelve signs of exactly thirty degrees is an arbitrary
business, and much depends on which point is taken
as the datum. An equally good case could be made for
assigning to Aquarius – and with him the whole zodiacal
system – dates up to 500 years later than those given here.

Yet there are signs that the critical moment is not so very
far off now. Already it may be that Aquarius is lifting his
teeming pitcher. Already, it seems, the Uranic birth-pangs
have begun. The ages are moving. And we, if we would
live, must move with them.

Man, however, has a natural inertia, a need for security.
Feeling that he must grasp *something*, he clings to the past.
For the future is not yet his to grasp.

And so we, the Pisceans, still nurture in our hearts the
spirits of former ages. Fervently the capitalist societies
preserve the worship of the god of growth. For Cancer
is a god who pays. Yet in the body of a converging world
the growth of cancer spells inevitable death. If one grows
richer it is because another grows poorer. Growth, too,

must be paid for. The body starts to prey on itself.

The heavenly Twins, too, are still with us. In the two-headed monster of church and state, in the Moses-and-Aaron cult of Marxist-Leninism, in political left and right, in 'men's work' and 'women's work'. Still the old symbols have life, and the dynamic of the Sacred Two becomes a promise of manifestation. A guarantee to deliver the goods.

Meanwhile the Christian world prefers to luxuriate in the warm bath of a Taurean saviour-mythology, true heir to the cult of Mithras.[143] It is by the vicarious blood and sweat of a heavenly redeemer, a convenient cosmic scapegoat, that mankind will somehow be saved. Man himself need lift hardly a finger. The appropriate words, the correct ritual, the approved form of belief – these alone will ensure the efficacy of the sacrifice. The faithful are saved by proxy, magically washed clean by the blood of the Bull.

Or, in Arian terms, by the blood of the Lamb.[144] For the spirit of Aries, too, is still very much with us. In the secular world no less than in the religious. The 'good society' is still one in which the leaders are trusted and the people do as they are told. The initiates must lead; the experts know best. The people, uncomprehending, must follow as best they can.

We are still the sheep. Still we follow the good shepherd. We may replace him from time to time. But always with another. For the Good Shepherd Concept remains our ideal. It is the model for our totalitarian dictatorships, the archetype of all our monolithic power-structures. It governs our politics, our trade and industry, our education, our religion. Still we are content to lie down in the green pastures of Aries.

Yet even the Psalmist of old realised that the sheep must move on.[145] Onward to those celebrated still waters from which life would spring. The waters of Pisces. Onward through the valley of the shadow of death, the end of the Piscean age. Onward to the celestial house where a banquet would be spread and where, in the presence of the Messiahs, the anointed ones, the cup of eternity would run over. Onward, then, to the house of Aquarius.

But what the Psalmist so clearly saw we are at best only dimly aware of. We ignore the passing of the ages. We defy the cosmic tide. So that when at last the rising waters breach the dyke, they will inevitably overwhelm our house of sand, and great will be the fall of it.[146]

The times are truly out of joint. Anachronism is the disease of the age.

For, if the ancients saw aright, the Piscean age should be an age of permissiveness. An age for the breaking of old moulds and accepted habits of thought. An essentially anarchic age for individual initiative, a new but more total Renaissance, such as only now is coming to the surface of human consciousness. An age for each fish to find its own level, follow its own path, pursue its own destiny. For if a fish is not free to descend, neither, by the same token, is it free to rise. And so it cannot take the celestial bait, and the fisherman of Pisces is thwarted in his task.

Yet from the point of view of the shoal itself, that freedom must inevitably spell suicide. If some fishes descend while others rise, then the cohesion of the shoal is threatened. The permissive society is a contradiction in terms. If it is a society, it is not permissive. If it is permissive, then the society itself must be destroyed.

Thus it is that the Piscean age spells the death of Arian society. And while those who value that society and its hierarchies may mourn its passing, yet there are compensations. For a society has no virtue in itself. Its value is the value of the individuals within it. And each has his destiny to fulfil. If, then, with the death of the shoal, the fishes are freed to pursue their several destinies, who shall bewail its passing? If our present society must die in order that true man may be born, then so be it.

Yet we should not forget that the Piscean fishes are still bound. Bound to each other by the law of karma. Even though the shoal lose its shape and identity, yet each fish is still linked to its neighbour. Let each fish, then, be guided by love of that neighbour.[147] For a fish that descends drags its fellows downwards with it. But, by the same token, a fish that ascends brings the whole race perceptibly nearer to the Light.

And that is the task of the initiates.

So Aquarius comes, bearing his heavenly pitcher before him. So the new age must begin with the rebirth of the initiates. In order that Piscis Australis[148]may gain his freedom, the caught fishes are returned to the sea. Judgement is poured out. The sword descends.[149] The stone of separation[150] is cast into the waters. And so on earth, too, the umbilical cord is eventually severed.

For the occupants of the pitcher are the angels of the judgement. They are the new midwives, the fishes who must gather the harvest of the deep, the fishes turned fishermen. They are the children of Uranus, the harvesters who must return to separate the wheat from the darnel,[151] the herdsmen who must divide the sheep from the goats.[152] The shining ones must sow division in order to reap eternity.

For this is to be the first harvest, the harvest of the elect.

Yet still it is the fishes themselves who really do the choosing. The Aquarian ruler does not need to resort to Arian coercion. The guests at the Banquet do not need to be locked in. The food and the wine themselves are attraction enough. The Light of the new dispensation is more than bread to them.

And so the new Messiah does not judge by what he sees or decide by what he hears.[153] *He* does not judge at all. Like the wise ruler of the Tao Te Ching, he knows better than to attempt to take the universe by force. Either the people follow his enlightenment or they do not. The decision is theirs.

Thus there are some who decline the invitation to the prince's wedding-feast. Whereupon the very highways and byways are combed. There is no tramp or vagabond but is brought into the Messianic Banquet.[154] The great net of Neptune is hauled up from the sea.[140] Every fish, every soul, must come up for judgement, lest even one should lose its vital chance. There is even more joy in heaven over the rescue of one lost soul than over ninety-nine who never got lost in the first place.[155]

Only now are the guests' credentials examined, only now are the fishes checked for size and quality. *Self*-examined, *self*-checked. The guests who have not provided a wedding-garment have already invited their own rejection.[156] The unwilling fishes are returned to the sea. But the willing fishes are gratefully delivered anew into the pail, the pitcher of Aquarius.[157] For the pitcher is both the beginning and the end, the Alpha and the Omega of the Aquarian age. In order that it may be poured out, it must first be filled. In order that it may be filled, it must first be poured out. The harvest is repeatedly ploughed back in.

For Aquarius is more than a fisherman. He is a fish-farmer. He is Uranus, who casts his children into Tartarus or Hades, shuts them up in the body of Gaea, imprisons them in the earth-planes.[75] But contrary to tradition, it is not out of hatred for them but out of love for its other inhabitants that he does so. If Aquarius returns his gleaming fishes to the sea, insists that the initiates, the *bodhisattvas*, descend again into hell, it is in order to rescue those that are still its prisoners. For that sea, that hell, is our world, and from it a new race must be born.

But at length the choice is made. The great gulf is finally fixed.[158] The gulf between the chosen and the rejected, the saved and the self-condemned, the Living and the dead. The Light is divided from the darkness, the uterine waters above the firmament from the waters below it.[159] The children of Aquarius are skimmed off. The children of Pisces are left.

Yet, physically, both are still children of their planet. Both, in their different ways, are still fishes. The bound fishes of Pisces; the freed fish of the Aquarian Piscis

Australis. And both must somehow co-exist. Aquarius has indeed spread a table for his elect in full view of their enemies.[160] For as this earth is the scene of the Banquet, so it is also the prison, the realm of outer darkness, the place of wailing and gnashing of teeth.[161]

Yet how is this separation to be achieved? What is the meaning of the Aquarian Banquet? What will be the nature of the new dispensation? What is the destiny of the chosen ones?

It is to be a new era. That, at least, is clear. The old order has collapsed, the old values have disappeared. And the new world, the Heavenly City, must arise on entirely new foundations.[108,109] A new earth under a new, Aquarian heaven.[162]

In particular it is to be an era of peace. The swords have been beaten into ploughshares, the spears into pruning-hooks. Each man may sit unmolested under his vine.[163] The acquisitive society, the ethic of getting (whether capitalist or socialist), has made way for the grace of giving.[176] An era, it seems, of simplicity and physical smallness, superseding the age of political giants and industrial dinosaurs. Man once more takes up his natural rôle vis-à-vis his environment. He attunes himself to nature, to the cosmos. He is cut back down to his true size. Small is beautiful.[164]

And in the process man rediscovers his own greatness. For he finds himself to be an extension of the cosmos and, by corollary, the cosmos to be an extension of himself.

And so, with the passing of the ancient Titans, the nation-state is no more. Each man is a citizen of the world. Where his inclination leads him, there he will settle. And, as is the way with birds of a feather, he will naturally choose to live with others of like mind. In peace.

Thus it is that the Piscean and Aquarian societies will co-exist on a single planet. For the spiritual gulf between them will be reflected in a physical symbol. The symbol of geographical distance.

With his own two feet, then, a man may choose his path of life. Attracted by the aroma of the Aquarian Banquet, any Piscean convert may apply for admission. Conversely any Aquarian guest who is sickened by the Banquet will be free to leave it.

Yet the Aquarian food and wine are not sickly by nature. Indeed, they are positively addictive. For we should remember that both are but symbols. Symbols of a greater reality.

Man does not live by physical bread alone, but by the bread of spiritual enlightenment.[165]

That age, certainly, will be one of physical progress and plenty, for the Pisceans no less than for the Aquarians. Perhaps, too, one of great technical achievement. But the followers of Aquarius, the citizens of the Kingdom, will have additional riches, additional food. Food which is itself a positive attraction, making unnecessary any negative restraints.

The *manna*, the bread from heaven, the elixir of Life.[166]

Led by the Aquarian avatars, the heirs of the Kingdom will be guided into all truth, and the knowledge of that truth will set them free.[167] Their minds will become pellucid as crystal, their consciousness transformed. 'I will pour out my spirit on all mankind,' says the biblical Jehovah through the prophet Joel. 'Your sons and your daughters shall prophesy, your old men shall dream dreams and your young men see visions.'[168]

Loosed from its ancient stall,[169] freed from the shackles and taboos of earlier ages, the human psyche will flower into the full splendour of gnosis. And the bees of the spirit, fertilising that flower, will carry off the pollen which is destined to produce the seed of a new cosmic humanity.

Bursting through the shell of the earlier world, man emerges from the womb into the sunlight. The true son of man appears in glory. Swinging down the ancient road out of the west, the new Arthur, invoking the ageless wisdom of Merlin, rescues the sword from the engulfing stone, the alchemist's gold from the dross, the spirit of man from its earthly prison. The human psyche at last realises its extraordinary potential. Mind starts to break free of matter.

And so now the fishes of Pisces cede their place to Piscis Australis[148] – the *single* fish whose task is to swallow the contents of the pitcher of Aquarius. For Aquarius is the Fish-Man[7] – the Sumerian Ea, the Babylonians' all-knowing Oannes – and both fish and man are present in his sign. The fishes of Pisces are assimilated into a larger body. From a merging of individual minds and wills a new, collective, transhuman consciousness is born. An autonomous, global being in its own right. A single entity, untouched therefore by individual birth or death. A New Man. An immortal.[170]

At first the individual human beings whose minds and souls comprise the New Man may be unconscious of his existence. They may notice among themselves only an increase in telepathic powers, in 'coincidental' manifestation, in 'instant karma'. Only later, perhaps, will the truth and the reality of their participation in his growing presence be fully accepted. Only later will they realise that Cronus, the heavenly successor of Uranus, is eating his own children, re-assimilating them into his body.[75] Only later will the heavenly archetype's power to transform mankind be realised and surrendered to.

But that surrender will come. The surrender that is the very meaning of *OM*, of *Subud*, of *Islam*. Thy will be done.[98] After the baptism of fire that ushers in the age,[85] the cosmic Christ will eventually arise like a towering phoenix[171] from the ashes of human will that are the souls of Aquarian humanity.

Christogenesis.[172]

And so both the Piscean and Aquarian dispensations bear fruit after their kind. The individual fishes give birth to more fishes amid the seas of darkness and mortality. And the sons of Aquarius are reborn as one in the living image of their heavenly father. They are transformed, transmuted. Through the alchemy of the spirit the base metal of humanity is turned to gold. The gold that has been refined in the fire.[85] Through the agency of the Kingdom, the New Man prepares to leave the world of matter behind and, crossing the cosmic Jordan, to enter the Promised Land of a new dimension, the planes of the spirit.

The age of Aquarius has become the gate of eternity.

And now we attend its dawning.

How, then, are we to prepare for that new age? How are we to ease the impending birth?

Only by a transformation of consciousness.

As Aquarius swings majestically across the heavens towards his celestial throne, our aim must be nothing less than a cosmic rendezvous. Peter must go to meet the approaching Messiah, must already start to walk upon the waters of mortality. And we, if we would help prepare the upper room for the coming Passover, the new dimension of consciousness out of which the Kingdom may grow, must actively seek out the heavenly water-carrier. Seek him out, then follow him. A positive initiative.

It is a question of attuning to the spirit of the age. And we attune by listening. Listening to the still small voice that echoes among the stars no less than in our own hearts.

Knock, and it shall be opened to you.[173] The *guru* is within.

Listen. And watch.

In the silence of deep meditation let the pool of our consciousness be stilled. As the waters clear, we, the Watchers, see into the depths of our soul. Now let the still surface of that pool become a mirror,[174] a reflector of heavenly Light. A mirror for the sun and stars. The sun that is at the gate of Aquarius.

So shall the soul become one with the Light.

Listen now, that the voice of Reality may speak. Listen for the songs of the moving constellations. Listen for the songs of Zion.

And attune.

Attune to the new song. Become one with your true self, with your fellow-man. Attune to all of nature, to the planet, to the cosmos. For you are it, as it is you.[175] All are one. Would you be the one wrong note in the symphony?

That listening is true prayer. Not a ceaseless catalogue of petty requests. Not 'What can God do for me?' but 'What can I do for God?' That through me the universe may grow. It is more blessed to give than to receive.[176] True prayer is the one word 'Yes'. The sacred OM.

Thy will be done. On earth as it is in heaven.[98]

Watch and pray.[177] Become aware.

Then act, in joy.[178]

5

Harvest Home

*Stretch out your sickle and reap; for harvest-time has come,
and earth's crop is over-ripe.*

THE REVELATION OF JOHN (14:15)

The Constellation Capricorn

The bearded one whose age begins in AD 4170 is Capricorn,
the Goat. He is the Hindus' Shiva, the horned madman,
lord of the cosmic dance of destruction and creation. He
is Pan, immemorial god of all nature, ever young and ever
self-renewing. Yet he is also Death who carries off all things,
and the source of things to come.[179]

For Capricorn's is the eighth age, the age of death and
continuing rebirth. With it one phase of the cycle ends and
another comes to life.

The ruler of the age of Capricorn is equally bearded. For he is none other than Saturn, the Ancient of Days. He is the Old One, Chronos, Father Time himself, for whom the passing of an age is but a tick of the clock in the night. He is also Cronus, son and heir of Uranus, whose children he rescues from their earthly prison with the aid of his sickle.[75]

And so the ancient staff that has served in turn as the wand of Mercury, the herdsman's goad, the shepherd's crook, the trident of Neptune and the Aquarian spear of Longinus, undergoes yet another transformation.

It becomes the sickle of the Reaper.

'Then as I looked,' relates John in his vision, 'there appeared a white cloud, and on the cloud sat one like a son of man. He had on his head a crown of gold and in his hand a sharp sickle. Another angel came out of the temple and called in a loud voice to him who sat on the cloud: "Stretch out your sickle and reap; for harvest-time has come, and earth's crop is over-ripe." So he who sat on the cloud put his sickle to the earth and its harvest was reaped.'[180]

And it is with the advent of the Capricornian Reaper, the Ancient of Days, that the world yields up that harvest. The first corn of enlightened humanity is safely gathered in. Cronus cuts short the age of Uranus and, leading his brothers and sisters to the light, succeeds to the heavenly kingdom.

But that succession entails an act of violence, even of savage brutality. The kingdom is not gained without a struggle. The gods of each succeeding age do not lightly relinquish their power. Yet, as the ancient peoples fully realised, the old god must die in order that the new may be born. As on earth, so in heaven, the seed must perish in order that the corn may sprout anew.

Thus, just as the Arian Moses must die before his people can reach their Promised Land, so the Piscean avatar must in turn assent to his own death in order to prepare the way for One greater than he. Hence the Way of the Cross. And soon, as we have seen, the world of the god of Pisces must in turn crumble into ruin before the approach of Aquarius.

It is a fixed decree of nature. There is no future in resisting the flow. An egg does not resist becoming a caterpillar, merely because it prefers to be an egg. And a caterpillar that attaches so much value to its caterpillar-nature that it declines to become a chrysalis does not become a butterfly. But then no caterpillar is so foolish. Caterpillars accept. And so butterflies abound.

Whence then, the resistance? Why is it necessary for Moses, the Arian avatar, to destroy the calf of Taurus? Why does Mars prolong his reign over the institutions of the modern world, threatening even to dispute the rightful claims of Uranus? And why will Uranus, the Aquarian god, in turn refuse to cede the kingdom to Cronus, his son and rightful heir?

The answer lies not in nature but in man – or rather in that aspect of man which sees itself as somehow at war with nature (as if he himself could survive for one moment if ever he won the battle). For we should remember the true nature of the gods, and of the signs of the zodiac themselves. If they have properties and characteristics, they are not of their own making. It is man who has brought order to the stars, man who formulates the laws of the universe. It is man who has named the constellations, divided up the heavens, assigned to each division a lordly ruler. It is man who gives life to that ruler, fashions his every desire and inclination, engineers his fate.

And so when Uranus resists the advent of his successor, it is not the stars, nor even the gods, that are to blame. It is man alone who, as foreseen by the ancient draughtsmen of the zodiac, is destined to resist the flow of the universe. And the more he resists, the more violent the eventual overthrow must be.

So it is that Cronus, wielding his Reaper's sickle, is forced to violence – to the act without which his brothers and sisters cannot escape their earthly prison, nor he accede to his rightful kingdom.

So it is that Cronus castrates his father Uranus.[75]

Now at last the symbolic blood and semen of human destiny can flow forward towards their goal. Now at last the Children of Israel can complete the first crossing of the cosmic Jordan, and the ripened corn of the Uranic age can be harvested and garnered. Not for nothing do the scriptures describe the Jordan-crossing as taking place at the time of harvest.[45]

No longer, then, is the harvest of Aquarius ploughed back in. No longer are the caught fishes returned to the waters. The time has come for them to be removed and preserved. They are ready to be eaten, assimilated, transformed into a new and greater body.

For now Cronus, as ancient tradition has it, must eat his own children.

Before we recoil in horror at yet another brutal affront to nature, we should further consider the meaning of the process we are describing. We are talking about gods, not men. And by gods we mean, not human beings who are somehow larger than life, magnified to the nth degree, but universal psychic principles, natural forces, climates of thought, the respective tempers of each succeeding age. If we have personified them, then it is merely in order the better to comprehend and memorialise them. Being ourselves human beings, we understand best what we can reduce to human terms. But if we think of gods as men, then we must expect some parts of the analogy to jar, just as we must if we think of them in terms of the planets which have come to bear their names. The gods are neither men nor heavenly bodies. Nor even gods, as popularly construed.

Thus, morality never enters the picture. We do not foist morality on the female spider who, in certain species, devours the male with whom she has just mated. We do not judge the young cuckoo who destroys its fosterparents' eggs, nor the mother who, in some wild species, will devour her own young. Nature, were it not 'red in tooth and claw', would not be nature. And are we to condemn the earth herself who, by means of her agents the scavengers, flies, worms and microbes, never ceases to devour her own children?

Cronus, then, by the same token, is in no sense the monster he is sometimes made out to be. His act is not even arbitrary, still less malicious. He eats his children because that is his destiny. That is what he was born for – or rather fashioned by the ancients. He is the great assimilator, the celestial matrix, the *Adam Kadmon* from which man came and to which he must return.

And return he does, with the advent of the age of Capricorn. Yet this is only the beginning of the process. At this stage it is only the *caught* fishes that are eaten – that is, the souls of the enlightened. Their escape from physicality and their subsequent assimilation into the Higher Self that is Cronus is due to their having attained a purely spiritual perfection. In a sense they have taken a short cut, a leap in the dark, by-passing those culminating phases of terrestrial evolution which their more earth-bound fellows have still to undergo.

Only Zeus escapes being devoured. Only Jupiter, in the hallowed tradition of the *bodhisattvas*, forgoes his immortality.

For earth remains.

And, swimming to and fro in the ancient seas of mortality, the uncaught fish likewise remain. Or perhaps even the Arian dispensation itself still lingers on, its pathetic flocks and herds still lingering fearfully on the brink.

But if so, then those flocks are much depleted. For the true sheep, the sheep that followed their spiritual destiny, have been removed. Only the goats remain.[152]

The goats of Capricorn.

Turned loose on the autumn stubble-lands of earth, Capricorn is the cosmic Goat. The Goat who is Pan, the god of all nature. With his advent even the denizens of Aries, it seems, at last learn to attune to the world around them, finally become one with nature. In the very heart of the physical they re-discover the seed of the spirit.

For the goat is not particular about what it eats. It finds its nourishment in all that is about it. Man, it seems, through his long exploration of the physical world, has actually come face to face with his own Reality, with the very source of the ancient wisdom.

The process has been a long one. So long, indeed, that nobody can tell when it began. Yet it was ultimately what man was born for – the reason for his whole terrestrial sojourn. The spirit of the universe, for reasons we can barely comprehend and in ways that we can scarcely guess at, stood in need of experience – an external experience which would enable it to see itself as it were from 'out there'. It needed a mirror, an image of itself to contemplate. And so man, as its agent, became the image of his soul, while the soul, for its part, risked coming to be regarded as the mere image of man – for who is to say whether object or image is the more real, or to decide which is dream and which reality? Losing itself in earthly experience, the human soul set out on the long path of Self-Realisation, the path which would eventually enable it to find itself again – but now a new, greater Self, immeasurably enriched.

Perhaps the process goes back to the very dawn of time, if dawn there ever was. More probably it is a recurring process, synchronised with the gradual precession of the zodiac. In which case the vital Self-separation, the crucial dichotomy, might be traced to a historical age such as that of Cancer or Gemini. Small wonder, at all events, that the process is associated astrologically with the Old One, the Ancient of Days himself, or that his age should have been symbolised in Egypt by the *ankh*, the very symbol of long life.

And so it is that the whole history of man comes to be portrayed as 'the ascent of man'. Not 'the fall of man'. Not 'the cycle of man'. Not even the Darwinian 'descent of man' – as though man's deeper nature had, like its physical vehicle, somehow descended from the trees. But his 'ascent' – the story of his long struggle to understand, cope with, and eventually control the forces of physical nature. The story of his science and technology.

Conventionally the story is traced through ancient Egypt, Babylon, Greece and Rome to the Renaissance, and thence to the science and civilisation of our own day. Other paths may be just as valid. But whatever the path, the story is the same. Little by little man discovers more and more about the world around him, as well as about himself in the physical sense. Little by little he unlocks the mysteries of chemistry, plumbs the depths of physics, probes the vastnesses of the stars.

And yet there is a curious anomaly. For the more he knows, the more he realises there is to know. As his knowledge increases, so does his sense of ignorance. The unknown expands in direct proportion to the known. So that when that day dawns when man's knowledge of the physical world touches on the infinite, he is faced with a sudden and shattering realisation – for in that same moment he realises that, in truth, he really knows nothing. And perhaps, indeed, truly knowing nothing is the ultimate in knowledge – the knowledge that, in Reality, everything is nothing, and nothing All.

And so it falls to Capricornian man to go forward towards the completion of the evolutionary circle. Admittedly, he has taken the long way around it, but then why else embark upon a circle in the first place? Arguably the merit and the benefit are even greater than in the case of the Aquarian 'elect' – those enlightened, spiritual ones who have sought the path of release, the quickest way out. By contrast, the zodiacal goats, the earthly remnant, have chosen the long terrestrial path – the essentially Piscean path which has left them free to explore. For the Babylonian Capricorn was always the Goat-*Fish*. Albeit by a different route, Capricorn heads in the same direction as Pisces. Via individual freedom towards total fulfilment. With the advent of the cosmic Goat, even the uncaught Piscean fishes approach their apotheosis. They have gone through hell and come out again on the other side. The ultimate initiation.

There in the depths of physical nature Man has rediscovered the very nature of Reality and, by the same token, the nature of himself. For the first time in millennia he realises his Oneness with the world 'out there', his truly universal identity. Thou art that.[175] Now at last the dichotomy of Gemini is healed, the duality of human consciousness finally resolved. Now at last there is only harmony and Oneness. Once more man takes on his ancient rôle as Pan. The tune of his pipes enchants the whole of nature, harmonises as of old with the cosmic symphony.

The son of man has descended into hell. Now he can rise again.

Yet the path is a long one. Idealism can grow cold. As he ages, Cronus too easily becomes fossilised, repressive, unwilling to move or change. Obsessively he clings for dear life to the *status quo*. Novelty is anathema, new thinking a crime. As paralysis comes to reign, the continuing development of humanity becomes blocked all over again.

The physical exploration of nature is all very well, but it carries a risk for the Capricornian explorers. The risk that they will come to assume that that is all there is. That everything is 'out there', that 'facts are all that matter'. With your eyes on the ground it is all too easy to forget that there are stars in the sky.

Yet sooner or later human beings have to sleep. Even in lying down on the ground, they turn their eyes heavenwards. And so at long last the penny drops. As the son of man nears the ultimate fulfilment of his destiny, he looks up in visions of the night. And there, in the patterns of the dancing galaxies, he sees his own image. That of a man coming in the clouds of heaven, who approaches the Ancient of Days and is finally presented to him.[181]

And it is the age of Sagittarius that is destined to see the lifting of that mighty dawn, the final reunion of man with his soul, his higher nature.

Sagittarius's is the ninth age, the age of total perfection (3^2). It is the age of the flying horseman. The celestial centaur, half-man, half-Pegasus, winging his way to heaven. And his coming offers the prospect of a miracle.

For once again the animal body is surmounted by a human head – indeed, not only the head but the torso and arms as well. Once again the symbols speak of the achievement of psychic wholeness, the harmony that was once that of Leo. And more than the harmony of Leo. For not only is the animal once more surmounted by the human, the lower nature brought into harmony with the higher. Not only is it once more a case of *mens sana in corpore sano*. That psychic reunion has been achieved by superior development of the lower faculties no less than the higher – the grace, the speed, the perfection symbolised by the horse. Capricornian man has found the seed of the Truth in the very heart of the physical. No longer, therefore, is the body recumbent, in repose. It is alive, vital, swift as an arrow.

The Constellation Sagittarius

The whole man seeks the truth, in heart, mind, soul and strength.[182] The four yogas converge upon perfection, the four paths lead to the summit of man's destiny. And in total union of body and spirit man in his new-found freedom goes forward to claim his eternal inheritance. The yoke, or *yoga*, that is perfect freedom.

And so the ancient goal of all religion is achieved. For religion is by definition a 'binding-back-together'. That making whole which is the characteristic of the holy. The Christian becomes one with his Christ, the Hindu becomes the *gopi*, the consort of Krishna. Individual man is reabsorbed into the Hindus' *Purusha*, the Hebrews' *Adam Kadmon*, the archetypal matrix of all life and creation, the *logos* or man-thought in the mind of God.

And yet it is not a matter of escape, the Hindus' *moksha*. That may admittedly at one time have been the nirvanic goal of the Buddhist, the age-long hope of the Christian that he might be delivered from the Evil One and from the fires of hell.[98] Nor is it a matter of mere separation, the Aquarian creaming-off of the elect by virtue of sheer spiritual enlightenment alone.

True, such paths have their merit, and are efficacious for those strong enough to follow them. The devotional path of the heart, the Hindu *bhakti*, whose badges are love and the desire for union with the Divine: or *jñana*, the path of the soul, of contemplation and meditation, the intuitive path of *gnosis*, of directly-derived Knowledge. Yet love and *gnosis* cannot be commanded, and are only marginally susceptible to the will. The path of love is open only to the natural lover, the path of *gnosis* to the seer. To all others such paths in isolation must inevitably seem too steep, and a slower ascent is needed.

And such is the path which, under Sagittarius, at last comes to fruition. The path of action, *karma yoga*. The path which is of the essence of man's karmic earthly sojourn, the very purpose of the terrestrial experience. No longer is it a question of escaping from the world of matter, of separating the spirit from its house of flesh – valid though that path may have been, in its due time, for those capable of following it. For to separate is to oppose, and opposition brings reaction in its train. Instead it becomes a question first of entering, then of transforming the world of matter itself, in the realisation that spirit and matter are mere polarisations of a single, unified Reality – and, as such, are largely illusory concepts at that.

The son of man must descend into hell. Spirit, instead of fleeing, must return to earth, [24] in order that, from the union, a New Man may be born. The concept is as old as the age of Gemini. It speaks of healing and of wholeness. It is the ancient message of Mercury, who is the herald of Jupiter.

Hence, then, the dispensation of Capricorn, with its submergence of man in the world of matter, the union of man with the natural universe, the plumbing of physicality to its very foundation. Until eventually that foundation is seen to be the self-same foundation that supports the world of spirit. The foundation that is Reality itself.

Thus it is that the whole universe, as the far-seeing Paul realised, is eventually to be transformed. For 'form' is no more than an attribute in the gift of man, a way of seeing, of organising the world as perceived. With the transformation of human consciousness that characterises the coming of Sagittarius, the universe too must undergo a metamorphosis – must be seen to take on new shapes, new functions, new attributes.

And so now, in fulfilment of the former Geminian dream, the ancient staff of the celestial archetypes at last becomes the thunderbolt of Zeus, sole surviving son and heir of Cronus. Long since proclaimed by Mercury, the prophet of healing, Jupiter the decisive ruler, the warrior, the thinker, the husband, the lover, the all-round god takes his heavenly seat. Jupiter, whose name means 'God the Father' or 'Sky-God Father'. Our Father who is in heaven.[98] The shaft of his enlightenment, in the hands of the Sagittarian avatars, finally shatters the tower of human consciousness, breaks open the fortress of mortality.[183]

And as the stone rolls away from the ancient tomb the New Man once more emerges – whole, entire, alive.

So man and horse become one. Spirit and body are reunited. The fire re-enters the stone. Duality gives way to unity. Sagittarius takes up his sacred bow, fits to it the single arrow of man's soul.

And fires.

And in that moment man finally achieves his ancient destiny. The arrow flies up towards the sun, pierces the heart of the cosmos.[184] Man becomes one with his creator. Union is achieved. The terrestrial cycle of evolution has fulfilled its purpose. Despite – or rather by virtue of – his physical wounds, the son of man, leaving his graveclothes behind, finally ascends into heaven. Man is made into the image of God.[185]

Apotheosis.

6

Winter Closes In

O lovers, O lovers, it is time to forsake this world.
The heavenly parting-drum comes to the ear of my soul.
Lo, the driver has risen and readied the camel-train
And asked us to indemnify him. Why, travellers, are you
* still sleeping?*

JALAL'UD-DIN RUMI (from *Divani Shamsi Tabriz*)

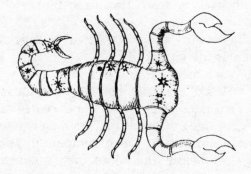

The Constellation Scorpio

AD 8490. The spiritually enlightened ones of the age of
Aquarius have long since achieved their destiny. Now,
too, the surviving Arians, through their achievement
of psychic wholeness, have been loosed by the bow
of Sagittarius into a welcoming eternity, gathering the
Piscean remnants on the way. In their thousands the
souls are withdrawing from incarnation. World population

decreases. Man goes to his long home, and the mourners go about the streets.

Now is the time when the pitcher is shattered at the spring and the wheel is broken at the well, when the silver cord is snapped and the golden bowl is broken. The dust returns to the earth as it began and the spirit returns to God who gave it. 'Emptiness, emptiness, says the Speaker, all is empty.'[186]

For now is the age of the Scorpion, the hour of the Great Beast.

The Scorpion symbolises physical death, and its sting is the sting of eternity. Yet that sting is none other than the ancient staff of the heavenly archetypes, which the physical now turns on itself. As ancient tradition has it, the Scorpion, faced with the fire, commits suicide. For man, death itself is dead, transfixed by the shaft of eternity.

'O death, where is thy sting?' asks Paul in anticipation. 'O grave, where is thy victory?'[187]

But Scorpio has a message, too, for the physical world which remains. It, too, must die. For Scorpio is the reverse of the Crab. Two ages after the commencement of the zodiacal cycle, the age of Cancer had been an age for life, for growth, for expansion. An age of rampant physicality.

Now, two ages before the same cycle's conclusion, Scorpio announces an age for dying, for withdrawal, for contraction. An age for the death of the physical. It is the tenth age, and man's destiny has been fulfilled. The tenth age, and eternity has been achieved. Now death must follow. For if there is no death, there can be no rebirth.

There will be other ages, other cycles. Other men.

Meanwhile the herald of the age of Scorpio is Mars. The warrior. The soldier. The returned centurion, Longinus himself,[126] whose renewed lancing finally releases the Sagittarian blood and water, the life-in-death, the last prisoners of mortality from the body of planet Earth. In his very sign (   ) we may see both the upward spear-thrust and the skyward-soaring arrow of the Sagittarian soul, the spirit of man as it re-penetrates the cosmos. The final resurrection.

Mars was always paradoxical. As the Greek Ares he acts both as rebel and as repressor. Having overthrown the existing order he will determinedly set up a new one of his own. For the sake of freedom he will impose discipline, for the sake of discipline fight for freedom. And from an irresponsible, churlish, vengeful, even sadistic youngster he is quite likely to mature into a solid, respectable, even noble pillar of society.

Small wonder, then, if paradox once again attends his acts now. For unknown to himself, it seems, Mars the repressor becomes, by his very act, Mars the liberator. The paradox is reflected in the very firmament. For the chief star of Scorpio is Antares, or anti-Mars. Perhaps it is a renewed attempt to impose the human will on the physical world that leads both to man's own physical death and to his triumphal entry into a higher form of reality. There is a titanic conflict between those powers now leaving earth and those returning to it. A conflict reflected in a renewed war of the elements. The eternal battle of ice and fire.

For now the ice returns.

Once more half a planet is laid waste by the icy fingers of the north. The works of man are ground to powder. All trace of the former civilisations disappears. Whole species of flora and fauna are wiped out. Any men still surviving retreat into the caves, migrate to warmer lands. All knowledge, all memory of the former world fades, disintegrates, disappears. The very elements of life are re-shaped, re-shuffled in preparation for a new cycle. A future new world.

And in the meantime the earth becomes a desert. As arid as only Ares (Mars) can make it. Truly the kingdom of the Scorpion.

And so the centuries pass. In silence the precessional sun burns its slow way across the waiting heavens. And eventually the earth – the still, spent, almost lifeless earth

– enters the age of Libra.

With Libra we once again approach the celestial fulcrum of the zodiacal progression. The great divide. One cycle dies, another comes to birth. A moment sacred to Venus, the morning and evening star.

And the sign of Libra is the sign of the Scales.

The Constellation Libra

The Libran era is thus an age for summing-up the present cycle, an age for judgement. It is the eleventh age, an age for realisation, for assessing achievement. The lessons are learned, the answers reapplied. In the spiritual sphere no less than the physical.

Like other signs Libra has its *alter ego*. It is the Dove.[171] For the Balance of Libra is the Scales of Horus, Son of Osiris, who is Judge of the Dead and Lord of Eternity. It is during the course of this earthly age that the souls of all mankind are destined to be finally judged. Weighed against a feather.

Let them show even the slightest weight, even the slightest imbalance towards the physical, and those souls must return. Return like those homing-pigeons, those celestial doves whose mission was to prepare them for this very judgement. Return to experience yet another cycle on earth, yet another zodiacal day.

But if they have succeeded in becoming weightless, pure, totally unattached, those souls may progress to a new plane of existence, a dimension of which we know almost nothing, where they may learn new lessons, undergo new cycles, achieve entry to even further dimensions of consciousness.[188] In perfect unity.

And the pointer of the Scales, the index of their accomplishment, the finger of judgement, is operated not by Horus, not by some independent divinity, but by themselves. It is their own weight, their own accomplishment that decides the issue. In succession to Ra, Horus merely pronounces the result. As ever, they are self-judged.

Judged by the staff of man's own destiny. For the pointer of the Scales is none other than the sting of Scorpio, the arrow of Sagittarius. It is the self-same ancient staff which, passed on from celestial archetype to celestial archetype, had eventually become the mind-shattering thunderbolt of Jupiter, the freer of man's soul. It is the emblem of office, the symbol of the changing function of man's own higher nature through all the ages. The analogue of the ancient standing-stone, it is nothing less than a shaft of heavenly Light from the eternal sun that is man's greater Self.

In view of this we can perhaps view with some tolerance – even, perhaps with approval – the priestly anxiety to portray the sun as dominating and controlling the symbols of each succeeding age. Anachronistic Leonism may not always be wholly to blame. The whole system, after all, is a direct function of the solar precession. Perhaps this is why the *uræus* of Gemini must be surmounted by the solar disc of Ra, the Bull of Taurus be overcome by the sun-god Mithras. Even the Lion of Leo must be tamed by man's Higher Self. And similarly, at the last, it is as Ra that the Divine Horus must pronounce judgement on the Libran soul of man.

And now, the weighing done, the judgement over, that mighty shaft acquires a new function. For with it the Virgin of human destiny is impregnated anew. A new house is prepared for the souls of the next cycle. Planted in the midwinter soil of Virgo, the staff must take root. The Glastonbury thorn of Joseph of Arimathea must send out new shoots, bring new life to the dormant earth.

Tabula rasa. A clean slate. A new beginning.

Once again the lowly god makes his way towards Bethlehem to be born.[189] The Winter Solstice is at hand. Life stirs in the depths of the Christmas cave. Soon the sun will return.

And so the circle closes. The day is done. For the remaining souls, the cycle recommences. But for those who have progressed to higher states, Hermes the *psychopompos* leads them on into new dimensions of experience. The thirteenth age is the first of a new cycle,[120,193] a further step in the ever-ascending spiral, the first note of a new twelve-note octave of cosmic vibration.

In Dryden's resounding words:

> *Through all the compass of the notes it ran,*
> *The diapason closing full in Man.*[190]

7

The Homecoming

In my Father's house are many mansions: if it were not so, I would have told you.

JESUS OF NAZARETH (Jn. 14:2 – A.V.)

And so the Magi return home. Their pilgrimage, like all pilgrimages, ends where it began. Like all pilgrimages, too, it is not the outer journey which counts, but the inner pilgrimage, the journey to the centre of the soul.

Yet those returning Wise Ones do not take the route by which they originally came. Having witnessed the new birth, deferred to the new avatar, they return home another way.[191] They complete the circle, commence a new turn of the spiral.

For spiral it is. Looked at in only two dimensions, the Cosmic Clock may indeed resemble a circle, a static symbol of non-progress, starting nowhere and finishing nowhere. But only to One who is already above it. Seen from the grass-roots level, from the point of view of struggling man, the Clock is nothing less than a gigantic spring, an evolutionary spiral, a cosmic snake whose coils, like those of a myriad mystic snakes throughout the ages, lead growing man ever upwards towards the Light.[192]

And who is to say what the next turn of that spiral will bring? For it pertains to another dimension, another mansion of the heavenly house, another cosmic estate. That it too will have its subdivisions, its stages of progress, we need not doubt. They may even be twelve in number.

But whether they or their counterparts on the future earth will mirror the features of the former spiral we cannot tell. It may well be that the Wise Ones of the next cycle will foresee another route, prepare other charts. And so man's higher nature, as reflected in the signs of the future zodiac, will take on new guises. New images will be projected onto the night sky for the benefit of such men as still remain prisoners of the physical world. The heavens themselves will put on another face.[193]

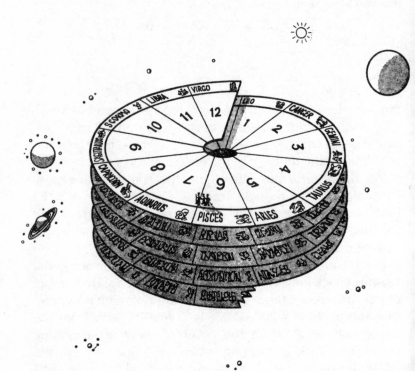

An exploded view of the Cosmic Clock – Man's stairway to the stars.

And so, consequently, will the Cosmic Clock.
But the rhythm itself will continue. The pendulum will

go on swinging to the rhythm of the turning planet, the changing seasons, the passing of the years, the precessional rhythm of the sun at the spring equinox. The rhythm of the ceaseless battle between ice and fire, between death and life. And to the tick of that remorseless metronome, the voice of man will continue to swell amid the cosmic symphony.

For man is central to that symphony. More than that, he is its conductor. It exists only to the extent of his own recognition of it, his awareness of its various parts, his responsiveness to its rhythms. The observed as a function of the observer, the known of the knower. Only in that moment when the knower becomes merged with the known does duality cease, and with it the world as we know it. Only when the last man forsakes his illusion of duality, the beloved delusion of his uniqueness and separateness, will the destiny of mankind be finally fulfilled, and the symphony take wing.

'Even by the mind this truth must be seen: there are not many but only One,' says the Supreme Teaching of the *Upanishads*. 'Who sees variety and not the Unity wanders on from death to death.'[194]

Wanders on, we could add, from cycle to cycle.

As the scribe of Genesis was to put it, 'while the earth lasts, seedtime and harvest, cold and heat, summer and winter, day and night shall never cease.'[195] So long as man observes duality, so long as he eats from the Tree of Knowledge of Good and Evil,[196] he remains man. And so long as he remains man his soul must undergo the continuing process of birth and death, of seedtime and harvest. The earthly process whose successive stages are reflected in the pilgrimage of the spring sun through the celestial zodiac, under each of whose twelve signs man must be born in turn. The twelve labours of Hercules.

Thus it is that, in the steps of the equinoctial sun, he moves from the midwinter of Virgo into the harmony of the Leonine spring, then onward into the growing-time of Cancer. Following the Geminian realisation of his dual nature, he must plant the spiritual seed of Taurus, graze the grasslands of Aries. Forsaking the shepherd's crook of the initiates, he must enter the dark waters of Pisces in preparation for the great rebirth of Aquarius. After the Capricornian harvest of the spiritually-enlightened, the remnant must then go on to seek a new apotheosis under Sagittarius, through the perfect union of physical and spiritual. For with Scorpio death once more walks abroad, and under Libra the achievement of the cycle is finally assessed. And so, as the sun re-enters Virgo, man completes one more stage of his cosmic journey, and a new initiative can begin.[197]

Such is the present cycle. Such is man's destiny. He may ignore it or misunderstand it. He may misuse its symbols, prostitute its knowledge. He may bend it into a mere tool for telling fortunes and predicting disasters. He may seek in it a source of oracles or magical power, failing to realise that true magic lies not in the stars but in man himself. Ignoring the very precessional movement on which the whole system is based, he may even attempt to classify people by the supposed sun-sign of their birth – a sign which, very often, is astronomically not even the right one.[198] In short, he may treat the stars as mere cosmic tea-leaves, stellar runes, galactic entrails. He may take the entire heavens for a crystal ball.

But he should not delude himself. For what he sees in the heavens he himself has already put there. The stars do not care. They are innocent. It is man himself who has imposed their masks upon them. And so man who seeks meanings in the stars merely looks into the minds of his ancient ancestors. It is their ideas that are out there among the wheeling galaxies. Immemorial visions that have nothing to do with magic or with fortune-telling, and everything to do with preserving the knowledge that is eventually to set man free. The knowledge that he has a spiritual destiny geared to the rhythms of the whole cosmos. The knowledge of his oneness with all creation. And no man can hope to do more than bring that knowledge back down to earth again. For once man knows, then he can act.[199]

Until, with the ancient Magi, he at last comes home. And then, with the twelfth age of 2160 years, another 26,000-year cycle of the zodiac is completed. With the twelfth month the Great Year draws to its close. Midnight has struck. Three hundred and sixty degrees are the measure of the celestial circle – the circle of man's destiny – and no less a number of days mark the span of the terrestrial year.

How long, then, is a day in those heavenly courts?[200] And how shall a man measure the degrees of the cycle of the ages?

He needs but live. And die.

For the three-hundred-and-sixtieth part of that mighty cycle is seventy-two years.

As the days of man are threescore years and ten.[201]

And so man, in his very life and death, takes up the rhythm of the eternal dance. His very consciousness resonates to the heartbeat of the cosmos. The child of man sits upright on a turning planet and, grasping the strings of destiny in his hands, draws together the purposes of the stars. Until eventually the microcosm is attuned to the macrocosm, diversity to unity, man to his Maker. Under the new-born Maestro, the cosmic symphony swells, and thunders on its way. And the ripples of its sound spread ever outwards through the galaxies until they are heard no more.

Man and the universe are One.

Part Two

Tableaux –
Symbol and Image

Introduction

The zodiac, it seems, is the means whereby the ancients, in a truly awesome leap of human imagination, contrived to write in the very stars the destiny of man. Part One of this book attempts to translate that same saga into everyday words, as represented by the black marks on paper which we call print.

Yet both star-pictures and print are no more than symbols. Far from being the truth itself, they merely stand for it. Nor are they the only symbolic systems whereby the message of the ancients can be expressed. For millennia its vital concepts have lain brooding in the depths of the human psyche, every so often rising again to the surface of man's consciousness in the form of legends and myths, of religious doctrines and systems, of dances and rituals, of painted or sculpted images.

It is to the presentation of a selection of those images that this section is devoted. Since they thus serve as 'tableaux' to what I have termed 'the procession of the ages', the images are presented in the same zodiacal order which governs the text of Part One. The story which there was told in words is here retold in pictures.

Virgin and Earth-Mother

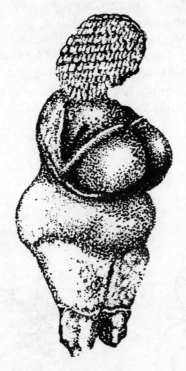

Among the earliest known examples of human sculpture are representations of generously-proportioned women who beg indentification with the primal Earth-Mother and goddess of fertility. Such is the so-called Venus of Willendorf (above). Zodiacally, her symbolism belongs to the period from the fourteenth to the twelfth millennium BC.

In Greek mythology she appears as Ge, or Gaea, the consort of Uranus (Sky) and the very embodiment of matter (*mater* = mother) itself. As such, she is typically coarse, fat, down-to-earth and unapologetically materialistic. Her sole functions are to conceive, to give birth, to nurse and to bring up her children – whence, of course, her physical characteristics as portrayed above. She can be generous, healing, protective and a reliable provider, but by the same token she can be murderously aggressive if her maternal instincts are thwarted, and especially if her children are threatened in any way.

Yet the Earth-Mother also has an alternative persona. Especially around the time of birth and infancy, and again later when the children are starting to grow up, she can take on the more spiritual character of the Great Mother of the Gods. Not that she is then without her dangerous,

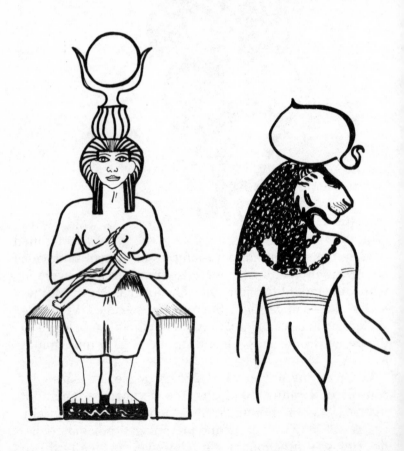

unpredictable side. But in this rôle she becomes the embodiment of such further qualities as idealistic love and self-sacrifice, of grace, intuition and sensitivity to the unconscious needs of others.

This general ambivalence is never absent from the universal tradition of the archetypal Mother. In the Sumerian Inanna, the Babylonian Ishtar/Astarte/Ashtaroth, the Phrygian Cybele, the Egyptian Hat-hor and the Hindu Kali especially, her negative side is as much to the fore as her more positive aspect. In the Egyptian Isis, by contrast, the accent starts to shift towards the more sylph-like and spiritual, and in the Christian cult of virgin and child this same aspect of her still predominates to this day.

During the late Egyptian period in particular, zodiacally anachronistic images such as that of Isis (opposite, left) *seem* to foreshadow the later Christian mythology, but in fact they represent very late survivals of a much earlier tradition. Indeed, in this case, the Divine Mother also bears upon her head the further symbols acquired during her passage through subsequent ages – namely the Leonine solar disc and the Taurean horns, both of which she has inherited from the similarly acquisitive Hat-hor. Meanwhile, in the illustration on the right (p 92), she is portrayed in almost totally Leonine guise, with the Divine solar disc of Ra upon her head modified only by the Geminian *uræus* or cobra, royal symbol of the inner wisdom.

Leo and the Tarot Pack

The Major Arcana of the Tarot pack comprises twenty-two images of great symbolic power and impact. Taken in sequence, the cards can be regarded as mapping out the evolutionary path of the individual human soul. Yet it is

XIX   The Sun

XI   Fortitude

by no means certain that they all derive from a single source, or that their sequence was always as it is now. Consequently any such spiritual correspondence must be ascribed either to sheer chance or to deeper forces continually at work within the universal human psyche. Similar considerations may well apply to the zodiac itself.

For reasons not unconnected with this apparent psychic undercurrent of continual change, the Tarot illustrations on the following pages are entirely modern ones that have been commissioned especially for this book. These contemporary versions by Pamela Jenkins are thus in a position to weave the various strands of earlier Tarot traditions into an integrated whole with some claim to universality. Moreover they have a modern idiom whose simplicity and directness helps to ensure that each card's symbolism is not masked by superficial irrelevancies of artistic or cultural fashion.

Thus expressed, many of the individual images bear a striking similarity to various of the zodiacal symbols. Card number nineteen, for example (opposite), is of obvious aptness to the age of Leo.

It is dawn. The rays of the rising sun strike powerfully in over a low garden-wall fringed by four sunflowers, and fall upon two naked children who are dancing, enraptured, within a magic circle on the grass.

The scene is Leonine in almost every respect. The rising sun, naturally, speaks for itself.[8] The wall of the secret garden begs identification as a *temenos* wall – the sacred boundary of almost any ancient magic enclosure. The magic circle is in the direct tradition of the stone circles of the ancient solar cults of the European Atlantic seaboard. And the dancing children – presumably male and female – speak vividly of man's total and unselfconscious oneness with himself and with the physical world around him. There is duality, admittedly, but a duality that is somehow at repose in unity, a potential but not yet actual polarity. Man having become as a little child, the kingdom of heaven is spread upon the earth.

As for the four sunflowers, these show themselves by their nature and number to represent the earthly equivalent of the celestial sun, the heavenly fire of developing knowledge and intellect which the age of Leo has brought down to earth. Yet the sunflowers are facing not the sun but the dancing children. It is *within them* – so the symbolism suggests – that the real Light of the World is to be found.

Meanwhile the eleventh card of the series, bearing the title 'Fortitude', supplies an even more obvious Leonine image. For here we have, in symbol, an exact counterpart of the Great Sphinx of Giza. The lower, animal nature –

represented by the male lion – is in repose, surmounted and totally controlled by the higher powers of spirit and reason. These are represented by the lady (clad in blue and white – the colours of heaven and of the clouds) bearing on her head a hat whose broad brim traces out the shape of the symbol for infinity (∞).

Also inherent in the picture is the image of woman as the great civiliser, the tamer of man's grosser, warlike instincts. Thus, at a deeper level, she is the *yin* which counterbalances the male-force *yang* to bring the polarities of existence into dynamic equilibrium – the equilibrium that is above all characteristic of the age of Leo.

Note, meanwhile, the historical aptness of the image. The more recent and familiar scheme of things conceives of universal duality in terms of a sky-father and earth-mother. In the present case, however, it is the sky-*mother* who dominates the earth-*father* – in the full tradition of dominant feminism which was the ancient legacy of the original age of Virgo. We find a clear echo in the primeval Egyptian myth of Nut, the sky-goddess, who descends in sexual embrace upon her brother Geb, the earth. (The same symbolism also seems to be belatedly reflected in the great megalithic sun-temples such as Stonehenge, where it is the uprights that penetrate the sockets of the sky-symbolising lintels.) It was not until the much later age of Aries (q.v.) that the alternative tradition of rampant masculinism was eventually to reach its zenith.

Cancer and the Moon

XVIII   The Moon

In the eighteenth card of the Tarot trumps we have an image redolent of the age of Cancer.

It is night. Out of the dark waters in the foreground a crayfish climbs onto the dry land. Before it a gloomy path leads towards a sombre horizon, while on either side two dogs (or a dog and a wolf) are howling at the moon, which is drawing droplets of water upwards towards it. Behind each animal a fortified gatehouse forbids commerce with the world beyond.

The Moon, as the ruler of the age of Cancer,[8] needs no introduction. The crayfish, closely related to the crab, is likewise an obvious symbol of the Cancerian dispensation. As it emerges from the depths of the sea, the source of life, a dark path stretches before it. It is the path of duality leading to Hades – the 'hell' implicit in physical existence – its twin, forbidding portals watched over, in the manner of the Egyptian Anubis, by their traditional canine guard. And the Moon's influence, unlike the Sun's, is seen to be negative, in conformity with its ancient rôle as the abode of the dead, as well as with Artemis's aspect as Hecate, goddess of witches.

Clearly the symbolism is sinister and threatening, and the imagery speaks clearly of man's fall into mortality and unenlightened physicality.

Gemini and the Hermit

IX   *The Hermit*

The ninth card of the Major Tarot trumps – the Hermit – provides an excellent illustration of the theme of the Geminian age.

An old man – apparently a monk – is making his way bareheaded along a dark and stony road. In one hand he holds up a lantern, shielding it with his cloak. The other hand grasps a staff, and up it a snake is climbing. In all of which we may detect distinct echoes of the myth of Hermes, the archetypal god of travellers.

But Hermes is far more than a mere traveller. As the spirit of crossroads and transitions, he is the great initiator, the wise man, the guru. And so we may identify the Hermit as the archetypal initiate, groping his way through the darkness of the world by the precious light of his mystic knowledge that is the Light of the World (compare the celebrated painting by Holman Hunt). His bare head is open to the elements: all his senses, in other words – including his higher awareness – are awake, on the alert. As always, the pilgrim's staff is for self-protection – as the rule of the ancient Essenes, for example, required explicitly. In other words, the Hermit must use superhuman force, if necessary, to protect his knowledge and ensure its successful transmission.

Already, then, the Tarot image of the Hermit foreshadows the rôle of the later, Arian initiates as typified by Moses – who was likewise to wield power by means of a 'magic' staff. The staff-borne serpent, too, was to have its counterpart in the later story.

Here, however, the snake springing from the ground seems to represent the serpent of the Outer, or Lower Wisdom: it, like the Hermit himself, peers forward into the gloom. For the Hermit's goal is its own goal too – its destined mate, the serpent of the Inner, or Higher Wisdom, representing the Knowledge that will eventually set man free.

At the same time the serpent begs identification with the sacred snake of healing that climbs the staff of the Greek Asclepius, mythical ancestor of all doctors and therapists.

But there is another mythical figure, too, whose staff comes into significant contact with serpents. This is the blind seer Teiresias, who as a result of this contact becomes first a woman and then once again a man. In the process he attains a lordly wisdom to which even the gods defer – a wisdom that is both feminine and masculine, both inner and outer, both lower and higher, both unconscious and conscious. It is this wisdom, born of the union of opposites, that is characteristically that of the age of Gemini. In the light of it humanity can hope to penetrate the darkness of ignorance and superstition, and so eventually to win through to the enlightened Sagittarian dispensation of Jupiter whose herald, Mercury, does indeed bear a staff, or *caduceus*, on which the twin snakes of the Lower and Higher wisdoms are eventually and triumphantly joined.

The Cult of the Bull

The historical cult of Taurus is perhaps best-known to us through the bull-cults of Minos, Assyria and late dynastic Egypt, though in almost all ancient cultures and mythologies the Bull had an honoured place.

It should be pointed out, however, that most of these cults represent no more than late survivals of a much earlier tradition. Zodiacally, the prime era for this tradition was the period from the fifth to the third millennium BC – precisely the birth-era of the Minoan, Mesopotamian and Egyptian traditions, and indeed of post-diluvian civilisation as such (see chart p.12). No wonder, then, that Venus/Aphrodite, with all her connotations of burgeoning fertility, should be its ruling goddess. It is from this era that the bull's head pictured opposite (left) probably dates – having been found in the royal tombs of Ur.

It is not altogether surprising, of course, that a high civilisation should continue to honour the gods which originally brought it to birth, for they were obviously its 'lucky stars'. Hence, perhaps, the late revival of Egyptian bull-worship which we know to have been in full swing at the time of Alexander the Great in the fourth century BC. The vast Serapeum at Sakkara (which he himself visited) and the Apis Bull illustrated opposite (right) both belong to this period, during which the dying civilisation, like all dying civilisations, was frantically searching for salvation in its ancient past.

Note, meanwhile, that the Apis Bull preserves on its head the symbols of even earlier ages – not only the Leonine sun-disc, but also the *uræus*, the restored 'eye of Horus' – the 'third eye' symbolic of the Hermetic wisdom proper to the age of Gemini.

The Cult of the Ram

The dynamic cult of the Ram-god, Amun, first arose to dominance in Egypt when Thebes became the imperial capital during the Middle Kingdom. Indeed, it was from the superseded Theban Bull-god, Mont, that Amun acquired both his tall head-dress (above, left) and his martial character.

This new development dates from around 2000 BC, the end of the zodiacal age of Taurus and the beginning of that of Aries. The Israelite Ram-cult, for its part, succeeded that of the Bull at around the time of the Exodus – or from shortly after 1500 BC. In both cases, then, religious developments accurately reflect the zodiacal precession.

Like other zodiacal symbols, however, Amun soon acquired the cast-off trappings of earlier ages. In the representation on the left for example, he bears the royal *uræus* or restored 'eye of Horus', Geminian symbol of the inner wisdom, and in time the priesthood was also to invest him with the solar symbolism of the earlier Leo, renaming him Amun-Re. Under Akhenaten this regressive process was to go even further, with an attempt to oust the Ram-cult completely, in favour of a monotheistic religion of love, based on the pure Sun-cult of Aten. Theologically, Akhenaten's revolution may have had much to recommend it; symbolically, however, it was born out of its due time, and the end of his brief reign not surprisingly saw the restoration of the rightful Ram-cult with renewed vigour and dynamism.

It fell to the Israelite shepherd-priest Moses, a century or so earlier, to perceive a more apt and durable way of reconciling the notion of the One God with the cult of the Ram. And in view of this one wonders whether the double head-dress of Amun-as-man (opposite, left) could have some hidden connection with the twin tablets of the Mosaic Law, the 'Tokens' which the Israelites were to preserve so jealously through all their wanderings and to which they were to attribute their very survival. The question acquires even further relevance, perhaps, when it is realised that Amun – the infuser of breath, or spirit, into the universe – was in fact the 'Hidden One', the self-same 'Unknown God' with whom St. Paul, at Athens, was later to identify Jehovah himself.

The Zodiac and the Avatars of Vishnu

Hindu tradition ascribes to Vishnu the Preserver ten avatars, some of whose characteristics reveal interesting and possibly significant similarities to received zodiacal symbolisms. They are:

1. The avatar of the fish (*matsya-avatara*), who saves the sage Manu from the great flood by providing him with a boat into which he is instructed to take a pair of each living species and the seed of every living plant. The obvious Noah symbolism (also found in the Babylonian *Epic of Gilgamesh*) suggests a possible Piscean or Aquarian context. (See the left-hand illustration above.)

2. The tortoise-avatar (*kurma-avatara*), whose activities seem to refer to the arising of multiplicity out of the observed duality of the universe.

3. The boar-avatar (*varaha-avatara*), rescuer of the earth-goddess from the waters. Historically, this might suggest either a Taurean or an Aquarian symbolism.

4. The man-lion avatar (*nrisimha-avatara*), who emerges from a stone pillar to slay the unbelieving demon-king Hiranyakasipu. Both lion and sacred solar megalith are clearly present in the story, thus suggesting the avatar of the age of Leo: and certainly there seems to be a distinctly solar aspect to his appearance as portrayed opposite (right).

5. The dwarf-avatar (*vamana-avatara*), cheater of the demon Bali and reconqueror of the three worlds.

6. Rama-with-the-axe (*Parashu-Rama*). Defender and avenger of his father the fire-god (Jamad-Agni), he eventually leaves the earth in shame. These details suggest a possible identification with the avatar of Cancer.

7. Rama-Chandra, superhuman hero of the *Ramayana*, and valorous saviour and restorer of his abducted wife Sita. The sheer Herculean magnitude of his deeds suggests a Taurean context, Sita perhaps representing the lost soul of man.

8. Krishna. Like Moses he is the survivor of a 'massacre of the innocents'. Spending many of his early years among shepherds (again like Moses), and having shepherdesses for his early consorts, Krishna then goes to war – the mighty war of the *Mahabharata*. Krishna thus reflects faithfully both the Arian and the Martial symbolisms of the Mosaic era, and identifies himself unmistakably as the Hindu avatar of the age of the Ram. His death, meanwhile, mirrors that of the legendary Achilles, wounded by an arrow in the left heel, his only vulnerable point.

9. The Buddha – here seen as a perverter of the ancient truth, whose teachings would eventually lead, in a roundabout way, to a new respect for the gods. Historically he, too, belongs to the age of Aries, though there seem to be Capricornian elements in his myth as expressed here.

10. Kalki. This final avatar of Vishnu, destined for an age as yet unborn, is portrayed as a giant with a horse's head who will close the age of iron and, wielding a fiery sword

like a comet, put an end to the wicked. His task done, the universe will then be reabsorbed into the primal matrix until the time comes for the next cycle to begin. Nothing could be clearer, in short, than that Kalki is to be the avatar of the age of the flying horseman, Sagittarius (q.v.).

The Piscean Fool

The Fool

On the face of it, there are few obvious connections between the Fool of the Tarot pack and the Piscean concept. Yet closer examination suggests otherwise.

The card is unnumbered. It shows a young fool, or jester, dressed in ragged clothes and pursuing a butterfly. On his shoulder he bears a bag or butterfly-net, and in one hand he holds a flower. Intent on his elusive quarry, and attacked from behind by a small dog, he is about to step over a precipice, apparently to his death. The mood, none the less, is summery and carefree.

The Fool may justly be identified with the common Joker – the 'anonymous' card which can transform almost any situation. Hence, perhaps, the lack of a number (indeed, he is traditionally treated as either the first or the last – The Alpha or Omega – of the whole sequence). For the Fool could represent the great avatar of any age – to his dog-like contemporaries, apparently a madman to be attacked and persecuted (an 'Idiot', as the Sufis would have it, or the 'scabby god' of the Aztecs), but a man of immense wisdom and power when seen in truer perspective (compare Paul at 1 Cor. 1:25).

In the present case, however, our perspective is limited by the frame of the picture. As in real life, we are too close to the Fool to understand what he is about to commit himself to. Certain things are nevertheless clear. The Fool, as we can see, is being lured onward to destruction by an elusive bait – here depicted as a butterfly. The same butterfly, perhaps, that to the ancient priests of Isis symbolised their own spiritual quest, their rôle as fishers and hunters for the souls of men. And it is this detail that immediately suggests a Piscean interpretation.

For, bearing in his hand the flower that is his soul, the Fool prepares, in his quest, to commit himself to a new element – the new dimension wherein hovers that equally flower-like goal that is the butterfly (Greek *psyche* = butterfly, soul, mind). On his shoulder he bears the instrument and symbol of his quest (or perhaps it is merely his 'cross', his burden of acquired karma). Just as the evolving Piscean fishes must emerge from their watery element into the air and dry land of the new dispensation, so the Fool too steps with supreme confidence from earth into the summer air in order that flower and butterfly may at last, as is their nature, become One.

The Fool, then, typifies the great leap into the unknown,

the voluntary giving up of physical life for something even greater and more Real, which is above all the trademark of the pre-eminent Piscean avatar, the cross-bearer of the zodiacal summer, Jesus of Nazareth. Perhaps, then, it is no accident that April 1st, the probable date of his crucifixion, should be known to us as All Fool's Day, or that the April Fool who is 'caught' should be known to the French as the April Fish.

The Star of Aquarius

XVII   *The Star*

The female figure represented in the seventeenth card of the Tarot trumps begs identification with Aquarius. She is a girl who, kneeling naked beside a pool or stream, is pouring water from two cups. That in her right hand she is emptying back into the pool, that in her left onto the dry land. Behind her, seven stars are shining in the sky: an eighth, larger than the rest, hangs directly above her head. In the background a dove hovers over a green tree.

The symbols need little introduction. The girl's water-pouring function is identical with that of Aquarius. Like him, her first task (that being performed by her right hand) is to return the water she has drawn (together with its Piscean contents) to its source. Her second task (that performed by her left hand) is to pour out the water and its contents onto the dry land. The seven stars speak numerologically of the spiritual perfection that likewise characterises the Aquarian seventh age. The eighth star, associated with the girl herself, marks her out for a Messianic rôle – the star having for millennia been the Messianic symbol *par excellence*. And meanwhile the dove, hovering over the distant tree, reflects the familiar Messianic symbolism of the ever-returning Holy Spirit and the mighty tree of the biblical Kingdom of Heaven.

The girl's nakedness – as in the tradition of classical Greek art – would suggest for her a godlike rôle. Her femininity, however, appears to contradict the traditional masculinity of Aquarius. Perhaps its purpose is to stress her apparent identity with Aphrodite, who is of course the daughter of Uranus. [8] Or perhaps it is merely that the Aquarian bridegroom-symbolism of the gospels is foreign to (and perhaps later than) this aspect of the Tarot tradition, which may have been influenced by the Virgan concept of the Earth-Mother from whose womb pour forth the waters of life.

Death, Devil and Capricorn

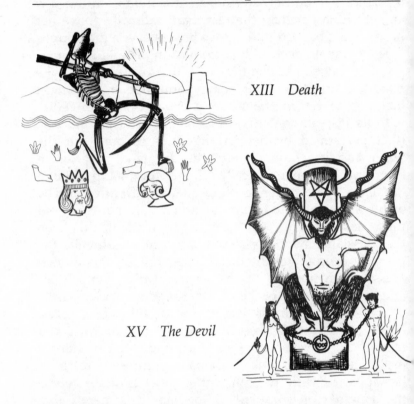

XIII   *Death*

XV   *The Devil*

Cards 13 and 15 of the Tarot's Major Arcana both seem to have clear relevance to the age of Capricorn. In the first, the familiar figure of Death is seen wielding his scythe. Severed heads and limbs lie around, yet seem to spring with new life from the very soil. In the background, the river Styx flows across the picture from left to right, and beyond it lies a gloomy realm where two great pylons frame the setting sun.

The central figure naturally recalls both Death himself and Old Father Time, but the living members suggest that his work, like that of Cronus, is not merely destructive, but regenerative too. Their destiny seems to be symbolised by the background. The setting sun suggests the end of the zodiacal day, the pylons some aspect of duality, and the distant landscape the land of the dead. When one takes into account the fact that an Egyptian hieroglyph (   ) seems to be incorporated into the picture, *and that this normally symbolised Libra*, the mystery seems to be solved. The 'victims' of Chronos do not die, but are consigned directly to the 'judgement' or assessment – the final weighing in the balance – that is to be the function of the age of Libra (q.v.), the concluding age of the zodiacal cycle.

Card 15, on the other hand, seems to refer to the destiny of those souls who remain. The central, androgynous controlling figure is the horned Pan – the 'Devil' of Christian mythology. Squatting on his stone plinth, he points downward with a commanding gesture towards the ring to which a male and female figure are firmly chained. Each has horns and a tail, and is thus identified as a true subject of the Kingdom of Hell.

Meanwhile both figures are so chained that the man can gain more freedom of movement only at the expense of the woman, and *vice versa*. Indeed, but for the presence of his or her partner at the other end of the chain, either could escape. Nothing could be clearer, in fact, than that their real jailor is duality itself.

Here, then, the symbolism speaks clearly of the destiny of the remaining Capricornians. Cast into the depths of nature, their imprisoned souls must explore physicality to its very limits. The fire is imprisoned in the stone. There is no escape for them. Their only hope of freedom lies in dragging the whole of hell upwards with them. They must learn to transform the very world itself. Only then can their long captivity end.

The Symbols of Sagittarius

I   The Magician

XVI   The Tower

Cards 1 and 16 of the Tarot trumps are highly suggestive of the Jupiterian age of Sagittarius, whose mythical embodiment is Zeus (opposite). Bearing aloft the instrument of his power, the Magician, standing four-square and self-assured, prepares to transform by his power the symbols of the four earthly elements. His wide-brimmed hat in earlier representations suggested the uniform of Odin, king of the Norse gods and pre-eminent Great Magician. Meanwhile above his head hovers the sign of eternity and the power of the spirit.

Card 16 shows the result of the process. A strong,

fortified tower atop a grassy hill is struck by lightning. Fire penetrates deep within. Its occupants are forthwith flung willy-nilly from the windows.

Here, then, we see the results of the Jupiterian initiative. The explosion of consciousness which it entails transforms the world of matter itself, destroys all former concepts and patterns of thought. Flung from what they thought was a fortress, the occupants at last realise that it was in fact their prison. Via the three windows, arranged pyramidally as the Sacred Delta, that symbolise the perfect manifestation of the Divine, the bolt of Zeus-Jupiter (the Buddhist *vajra*) blasts them to freedom and immortality, as in the Greek tradition, and stands their whole world on its head.

These and other resemblances between Tarot, zodiac, traditional numerology, Qabalah, Classical mythology, Hebrew alphabet and other symbolic systems have tempted some researchers to suggest that all in reality are identical and therefore mutually interchangeable. Their attempts to devise a single, rigid, 'total' matrix have generally tended, however, to do violence to the systems involved. No doubt all the systems do portray in some way the path of the soul: possibly all begin at the same point and lead to the same goal. But it is stretching probability to suggest that all must therefore proceed in the same order and by the same steps. Indeed, the evidence suggests that, while certain steps are certainly common to a number of systems, the various traditions listed probably grew up largely independently, as spiritual paths in their own right, and have since become more closely interrelated by a simple process of cross-fertilisation.

The Twin Kingdoms of Scorpio

III   *The Empress*

IV   *The Emperor*

The third and fourth cards of the Tarot's Major Arcana seem to point to the two alternative finalities characteristic of the age of Scorpio.

The Scorpion itself does not appear in the Tarot's gallery of symbols, and even outside it the image appears but rarely. It is as though the advent of the age of Scorpio is a thing to be dreaded, an event to be spoken of in hushed tones, if at all. For to speak of Scorpio is to speak of Death, and to speak of Death is to invite Him to appear.

In deference to the ancient taboo, therefore, it is as the Eagle, his traditional *alter ego*, that Scorpio more often appears – the soaring Eagle which represents man's soul enthroned in nature, triumphant over the gravity of the very physical world from which it has sprung. For this, too, is one part of the destiny of the age of Scorpio.

And so it is on a square throne emblazoned with the Eagle that the Emperor of the fourth card sits (opposite, left) – the self-same Eagle which has been adopted as a device by warlike and militaristic states almost without number through the ages. For the Emperor is a despot. That much is clear from the world-symbolising orb which he bears in his right hand and the phallic sceptre, with which he dominates it, in his left. Indeed, this very left-handedness could be taken as indicating, in symbol, his 'sinister' nature. And as if these trade-marks were not sufficient, he bears on his clothing the symbols of Aries, whose ruler, like Scorpio's, is Mars.[8] In short, he is none other than the returned Martial archetype, the organiser, the deviser of rigid systems, the repressor, the codifier, the go-getter, the masculine personification of rampant human will.

No doubt such qualities have their place. They were appropriate above all to the age of Aries. But in the Emperor we see the result of their prolongation beyond their cosmic time. By the obsessive exercise of his will man can indeed conquer his environment and win the battle against nature – but the result, as the card shows quite clearly, can only be a desert. The world-desert of the age of Scorpio. And so man, through his determination to become Emperor of the physical world, destroys the very empire over which he would rule. But for the reigning taboo, his device should indeed be the crawling Scorpion, not the Eagle. The Emperor is left sitting on his throne on the bare mountainside, monarch of all he surveys. Monarch of nothing.

It is an irony of almost tragic proportions that so many greedy and militaristic states throughout history have borne as their proud device the aquiline substitute-symbol of that very world-devastation to which general acceptance of their basic philosophy must inevitably lead. Nations and movements even today not uncommonly betray through their favourite symbols a subconscious knowledge of their eventual destinies. Representative of them, perhaps, are those countries and movements who by adopting as their symbols the sickle of Saturn and the hammer of Thor (that is, the bolt of Jupiter) proclaim a direct allegiance to the physically-orientated dispensation of Capricorn and Sagittarius.

The Empress of the third card, meanwhile, demonstrates the alternative finality (p. 114, right). She, too, is identified by the aquiline shield of Scorpio. She, too, bears a sceptre. But this time the device of the Eagle is (as we shall see) properly used. The sceptre is here none other than the Virgan ear of corn, and she herself is clearly none other than the primal Earth-Mother, the archetypal Virgo. It is no more than appropriate, therefore, that about her head revolves a diadem of twelve stars – the twelve signs of the very zodiac of which she herself is the beginning and the end, the Alpha and the Omega. Thus adorned, she personifies attunement to the flow of the universe, harmonious acceptance of the tide of evolution.

From the card we can see the result of that attunement and acceptance. The growing-time of the zodiac has at last borne fruit, the evolutionary process has fulfilled its work. The perfection symbolised by the card's very number has been achieved. As the sun sets over an autumn earth, the universe pours out its cornucopia of ripened fruits at the feet of humanity, deferring to mankind as the new lord of creation in final fulfilment of the Genesis-story. And it does so because humanity has found in the very womb of the Earth-Mother the seed of the spiritual. Through man's experience of, and surrender to, the nature of which he is part – through that acceptance and receptivity typified by the Empress's reclining form, in contrast to the Emperor's wilful self-assertiveness – he has come to know both physical and spiritual to be but twin manifestations of a single eternal Reality. And it is in that knowledge, that Realisation, that the Scorpionic soul can at last soar heavenwards, borne aloft on veritable Eagle's wings.

The Judgement

The essentially Libran 'vision of the judgement' usually ascribed to Christianity has in fact a much older pedigree. In the Osirian tradition it was already thoroughly familiar to Egyptians of the second millennium BC, as this painting from a Twentieth Dynasty funerary casket testifies.

After the deceased has recited the celebrated Negative Confession of Innocence and answered the questions of the Forty-Two Assessors, his heart (or soul) is weighed (right) against the goddess Maat – the Egyptian equivalent of Tao, Dharma or Universal Law. On her head is her symbol, the ostrich-feather, in accordance with the ancient tradition

that the soul must achieve feather-like weightlessness –
total purity – if it is to inherit the bliss of the eternal planes.

In charge of the weighing is Anubis, the dog-headed
guardian of the dead who is associated with Sirius the Dog-
Star and thus with the divine Isis herself. Thoth, the ibis-
headed god of learning, records the result.

On the left, Horus-as-Ra fulfils the rôle of his father
Osiris, whose karmic regalia (crook, flail and *djed*-column)
he bears. And so, as in the Christian tradition, it is the
Son of God who pronounces the ultimate verdict, finally
bringing the souls of the redeemed before the eternal
throne.

Journey's End

XX1   *The World*

The last card of the Tarot's Major Arcana (if we except the Fool) is The World. It shows a reportedly androgynous figure floating, as it were, in the void. In its hands are two flaming wands, and around it an egg-shaped wreath. Wrapped about its body is a drape that seems originally to have represented the serpent of the Inner Wisdom. In the corners of the card are to be seen the four ancient tetramorphs – Man, Lion, Bull and Eagle. The whole picture is a direct reflection of a favourite Mithraic image showing Mithras, the Conquering Sun, triumphant over the cycle of the zodiac.

This last card of the sequence reflects the conclusion of the human evolutionary process. Floating at the still centre of the world-egg, the wheeling cosmos, man has achieved his destiny. No longer is he male or female, no longer is he subject to the world of opposites. Instead, he himself has become undisputed master of the twin wands of duality, guardian of the powers of positive and negative.

As if to confirm his achievement, this final equilibrium, the four tetramorphs encircle him. Biblically they are the symbols of the four gospels – Matthew, Mark, Luke and John (in that order). Astrologically, they are said to mark the four 'cardinal signs' of the zodiac – Aquarius, Leo, Taurus and Scorpio respectively (the Eagle having long been regarded as the *alter ego*, the positive aspect, of Scorpio).

In this card, then, man's final triumph is made explicit. No longer is he subject to the present evolutionary spiral of the zodiacal precession. He has himself become its centre, the axis about which it revolves, the universal Sun, the source of all life and power. He has become One with the Prime Mover, the Original Cause, the Cosmic Infinitive. Under the terms of the known zodiac, there is no more to be learnt, no more growing to do. The goal of Divinity has been achieved.

Notes and References

Notes and References

(Abbreviated references in Roman type, unless otherwise indicated, are to the New English Bible).

1 Matt. 2:1–12.
2 It could be significant, for example, that many of our terms for mental and spiritual states and processes are taken from ancient Greek.
3 The idea was almost universal among the ancient philosophers of both East and West – most notably, perhaps, in the case of the tradition which produced the celebrated *I Ching*, the *Book of Changes* upon which both Lao Tzu and Confucius are reported to have based much of their wisdom.
4 Commonly quoted as the motto of the so-called Hermetic school of philosophy.
5 See, for example, Rhodes W. Fairbridge's research into the polar ice cycle and its effects in *Scientific American*, May 1960, Vol. 202, No. 5. This astroclimatic process is normally known by climatologists as the 'Milankovitch Model', after the scientist who first proposed it.
6 The so-called cycle of the equinoctial precession.
7 Compare 2 Esdr. 14:11–18 and especially verse 11. In some Eastern traditions the sky is differently divided, and even in the Middle Eastern version some of the signs 'merge' to some extent. To the Babylonians, for example, there were three 'fish-signs' – Pisces, Aquarius (the Fish-Man) and Capricorn (the Goat-Fish) – all of which could thus be regarded as separate aspects of a single sign.
8 Compare the chart of the Cosmic Clock, p.2.
9 A period of 4320 million years is quoted by Mme. Blavatsky (*The Secret Doctrine*, Theosophical University Press, 1888) as the length of the traditional Hindu 'Day of Brahma', the universe's 'outbreath': the corresponding 'inbreath', or 'Night of Brahma' is said to be of equal length. In these terms the cycle completes itself every 8640 million years.
10 Compare Isa. 7:14, Matt. 1:20–23, Lk. 1:26–38.
11 Compare Matt. 1:23.
12 Plato: *Timæs* and *Critias*.
13 See the chart of the Cosmic Clock (p.2). Astrologically the sun is traditionally regarded as the 'ruler' of the sign of Leo. The other 'rulers' are likewise indicated on the chart.

14 Compare the circular carved zodiac from the temple of Hathor at Dendera, now in the Louvre, Paris. Although supposedly dating from 34 BC, this shows the sky as it was in 700 BC or earlier, possibly suggesting that it is a copy of similar works of Sargon's time (see R.H.Allen: *Star Names, Their Lore and Meaning*, Dover, 1963). Here the four 'cardinal points' of the zodiac are clearly marked by the four pairs of supporting deities, and two of those cardinal points correspond to obvious vertical alignments of the internal figures. The line corresponding to the beginning of Gemini passes directly through the column of figures in question, while that marking the commencement of Leo passes immediately *to the left* of its associated column, and thus through almost the only empty radial 'corridor' on the zodiac. Significantly, however, the line does pass through one small feature – and that is none other than the outstretched arm of Virgo, bearing its 'ear of corn'. No more apt symbolism could surely be found for the beginning of a new cycle. (Compare the partial representation below.)

Two further markers on the rim of the original design also mark the ages of Scorpio and Taurus, thus apparently defining, in the latter case, the historical foundation of Egypt, or even of post-diluvian civilisation as such. Schwaller de Lubicz also claims to detect a dating corresponding to the early Piscean age, which is known to have seen the temple's final reconstruction. The temple's original, however (on the evidence of its own inscriptions), owed its design to none other than Imhotep, son of Ptah and rumoured designer of the earliest pyramids.

15   Josephus: *Wars of the Jews*, Book II, viii, and compare the Qumran Hymn-Scroll, sections 7, 14, 19 (Tr. G. Vermes in *The Dead Sea Scrolls In English*, Penguin, 1962).

16   Compare Rutherford: *Pyramidology* (Institute of Pyramidology, 1957 onwards) and Lemesurier: *The Great Pyramid Decoded* (Element, 1977).

17   Compare Gen. 6:1, 9:1.

18   See Gen. 6:3, and compare p.97.

19   According to Plato (*op. cit.*), the first kings of Atlantis were five pairs of twins, the sons of its founder, Poseidon.

20   Ex. 4:16.

21   An enlightened and compassionate one who, in the Buddhist tradition, voluntarily delays his own entry into Nirvana until all other sentient beings have likewise attained enlightenment.

22   That allegorical task being still incomplete, Moses never in fact reaches the Promised Land (Deut. 34:4–6).

23   Numbers 21:6–9. Compare the symbolism of the Tarot on page 98.

24   Compare the imagery of the so-called *Emerald Tablet of Hermes* and the Mayan *Chilam Balam of Chumayel*.

25   Compare Lk. 15:11–32, a story which seems to symbolise the very nature of man's terrestrial experience.

26   Matt. 10:16.

27   In the Genesis creation account, too, the inception of the age of agriculture is linked with the eating of the symbolic apple (3:1–19). Meanwhile compare p.100.

28   The golden age of Egyptian pyramid-building is usually dated at around the middle of the third millennium BC.

29   Ex. 12:1–20. Compare pp.102 and 105.

30   Ex. 20:1–17.

31   Ex. 32:15–35.

32   See Schonfield: *Those Incredible Christians* (Bernard Geis, 1968). Comparison of Matt. 12:11 with Lk. 14:5 supplies clear, if accidental, corroboration of the ass/ram thesis, and suggests that the knowledge of this symbolic interrelationship was still alive as late

as the first century AD.

33 Compare the star-map on page 28. *The Triangle* is certainly an odd name for a constellation. It could, after all, equally well be applied to almost any group of three stars. Why, then, apply it to these three in particular? One possible explanation could be that the Triangle was simply intended as a kind of anonymous substitute-sign, rather like the joker in a pack of cards, or like one of the substitute flags in sea-signalling (all of which, oddly enough, are triangular). In which case its rôle would aptly parallel that apparently assigned to the Ass by occult tradition as the substitute-symbol for the Ram. Yet Set was always seen specifically as the *negative*, or '*dark* aspect' of Horus. Consequently it may be that the name *Triangulum* represents a deliberate piece of dissimulation on the part of the ancients – as though the constellation's real meaning were in some way unspeakable; some sinister, negative telluric force to be referred to in awe and trembling, if at all.

Triangulum's close celestial proximity to the constellation Aries (in whose sign it therefore properly falls) would seem to support this view of the suggested link. In fact, we may perhaps see the constellation's inverted triangle (∇) as signifying all the most deeply negative and threatening aspects of the Arian dispensation. In which case, if the archetypal positive symbol of Divine manifestation on earth was traditionally the pyramid or delta ($\triangle$), is it any wonder that the Hebrew sign of the Messiah, conqueror of the Powers of Darkness, the Son of David as he drew near on his symbolic donkey, was always ✡ ?

Further support for the Typhonian interpretation of this constellation may be claimed from the fact that Triangulum was regarded by the ancients as the celestial counterpart of the equally three-cornered island of Sicily – *Sicilia* was indeed one of the constellation's own titles – an island which, according to Classical tradition, owed its very existence to the fact that Zeus, in a desperate moment, flung its rocks and mountains upon his mortal foe, Typhon, who now lies imprisoned beneath the very roots of Etna's volcano.

As against this view, however, it is known that an early tradition – possibly familiar to the author of Zech. 9:9 – associated 'the Ass and its Foal' with the constellation Cancer, whence conceivably the apparent confusion in later years as to whether Jesus rode on one donkey or two into Jerusalem (compare Mk. 11:1–7 with the later Matt. 21: 1–7). In these terms, the zodiacal symbolism of Jesus' act would then presumably refer to his victory over man's earlier fall into Cancerian physicality, an initiative reflected in the essential spirituality of his message.

34   Zech. 9:9. The prophet's requirement is not only extraordinarily impractical but highly specific and dogmatic – and this fact alone should alert us to the possibility that some deep symbolic process is at work.

35   Meanwhile the first letter of the Hebrew word *ayir* (**ע** – formerly written **Y** , and thus apparently cognate with the Typhonian ass-symbol, **Y**) is itself called *ayin*.

36   Lk. 2:8–20, and compare Isa. 1:3.

37   Jn. 8:12, 9:5.

38   Luke 1:78. The evident solar symbolism of the Nazarene initiative may help to explain why the ideas of Plato, himself an initiate of the Apollonian sun-cult, should have proved so seductive to Jesus' later followers (thanks notably to the Neoplatonists of Alexandria), so helping to bring about a considerable influx of Greek ideas into Christian thought. Significantly, perhaps, the *Mithraic* sun-cult was also to exercise a considerable, even overwhelming influence.

39   Matt. 2:9.

40   Matt. 3:13–17, Mk. 1:9–11, Lk. 3:21–2, Jn. 1:24–31.

41   Josephus: *Wars of the Jews*, Book II, viii. (Tr., A. Powell Davies in *The Meaning of the Dead Sea Scrolls*, Mentor, 1956.)

42   *Brihad-Aranyaka Upanishad*, 1.3.28 (Tr., J. Mascaró in *The Upanishads*, Penguin, 1965).

43   Gen. 6–8.

44   Ex. 14.

45   Josh. 3–4.

46   Compare Rev. 3:1, Jn. 5:24–26, 1 Cor. 15:20–58.

47   Matt. 3:16–17, Mk. 1:10, Lk. 3:21–2, Jn. 1:32

48   Gen. 8:8–13.

49   Bethlehem = 'place of bread'.

50   Matt. 6:11, Lk. 11:2. The word here rendered as 'daily' is a traditional source of difficulty for translators. 'Supersubstantial' probably represents the best available rendering.

51   Matt. 14:13–21 and 15:32–8, Mk. 6:34–44 and 8:14–21, Lk. 9:12–17, Jn. 6:1–13.

52   Matt. 26:26, Mk. 14:22, Lk. 22:19.

53   Matt. 15:27, Mk. 7:28, Lk. 16:21.

54   Jn. 13:21–30.

55   In the Roman arena it was usually the *murmillo* who was pitted against *retiarius*, the trident-bearing net fighter. Armed with sword and shield, *murmillo* wore a Gallic helmet whose crest bore the image of a fish.

56   Matt. 13:47–50.

57   Matt. 22:14.

58   Matt. 4:18–22, Mk. 1:16–20.

59 See the Hymn numbered 8 by Vermes (*The Dead Sea Scrolls in English*, Penguin, 1962).

60 Both Burrows and Allegro report zodiacal commentaries in Cave Four at Qumran.

61 Matt. 4:19, Mk. 1:17.

62 See note 51 and compare, for example, Matt. 14:13–21 and 15:32–38.

63 Rev. 14:1.

64 See Matt. 16:5–12.

65 Matt. 5:17.

66 Compare Jn. 5:25.

67 Mk. 4:35–41.

68 Lk. 5:4–11, Jn. 21:5–7.

69 Jn. 21:6.

70 Lk. 5:1–3.

71 Matt. 14:22–33.

72 See, for example, Isa. 9:4, 10:27, 25:9, 49:9, 58:6.

73 Jesus never seems to have been quite sure which age he himself really belonged to. Not that there was any doubt in his mind that he was living and working in a basically Piscean context. But his real kingdom, as he himself put it, was 'not of this age' (compare Jn. 18:36); his whole mission was dedicated to the proclamation of another age, a future world, the Aquarian Kingdom of Heaven, in which he himself would return to rule in Uranic splendour. It is as though he somehow regarded himself as existing *outside time* – as one might perhaps expect if he was truly living directly from the Divine *ruach*, the Holy Spirit.

Jesus. in short, was both Alpha and Omega, the first and last (see Rev. 22:13); that is, he was both A/∝ (a form of ⟨ / ඊ , the bull-sign of the pre-exodic Taurus) and Ω, which begs identification with the reversed pitcher of Aquarius. Already present, perhaps, in Abraham and Moses, he had incarnated now as the prophetic forerunner, the avatar of the age of preparation, the 'man made in the image of God' of the sixth day of creation. Having become both priest and offering, he would then in due course reappear to reap the fruit of his earlier work for humanity, and to share with his Creator the joy of the Cosmic Sabbath. And so he would finally fulfil the apparently irreconcilable biblical requirements that the One Who Should Come should be not only Prophet, but also Priest and King.

Curiously enough, however, Jesus seems not to have looked beyond the age of Aquarius, the seventh age, as though that was indeed to mark the Sabbath, the conclusion of his mission. And given that his own destiny was expressly wrapped up with that of Israel itself – as though he were, in a sense, an incarnation specifically of its own 'group-soul', its own 'guardian angel' – one has the impression that it was to mark the end of his nation's mission, too. For them it was to be the Last of the Ages, the swansong of the initiates, the Hebrew Grand Finale. Zodiacally the next two ages on earth (q.v.) seem to be the province less of Jesus than of Pan – from among whose humble subjects the mighty centaur Sagittarius is destined eventually to arise. It may be, then, that the mission of Jesus, as he himself suggested (Matt. 15:24), was specifically to the house of Israel – a limited planetary initiative on the part of the greater Cosmic Christ, specific to one-third of the zodiacal cycle, the four ages from Taurus to Aquarius.

Or could it be that the Omega sign has a dual function? Could it be that it also points directly to a new dispensation of Leo[8], a further Golden Age in another dimension entirely, the first room of many in a new and heavenly mansion? (Compare chapter 7.)

74   Jn. 2:1–11.

75   The extraordinary Greek tradition related by Hesiod tells how Gaea (Earth) gave birth to Uranus (Heaven), by whom she then bore a number of children. Out of hatred for them, Uranus shut them up in her body (or alternatively in Tartarus, or Hades), where one of them, Cronus, organised a revolt. Succeeding in his escape-plan, he castrated his father Uranus with a sickle, and took over as king of the heavens. Subsequently, however, he proceeded to eat his own children, of whom only Zeus, his eventual successor, escaped. Nothing could be clearer, of course, than that these various happenings are highly symbolic and dreamlike, in much the same way as are the zodiacal signs themselves.

76   See, for example, Ps. 23:5, Isa. 25:6–8 and Matt. 22:1–14.

77   Matt. 12:11–12, Lk. 14:5–6. Note again that, in Luke's account, it is the *donkey* or the ox that is referred to, while in Matthew's it is the *sheep* that may be rescued from the well – a variation which reflects the interchangeability already referred to. The Essenes' *Damascus Rule* specifically forbids such 'sabbath rescues', however.

78   Jn. 4:14.

79   Matthew, 19:28: the expression (a reference to Isa. 65:17f) is often translated into English as 'the world to come'.

80   Jn. 3:3.

81   Isa. 26:19.

82   Jn. 3:1–21.

83   Matt. 18:3. The translators often have difficulty with this expression: the would-be heirs of the Kingdom must variously be 'converted', 'transformed', 'turned around' or must 'become as' little children. Such undignified squirming by translators generally indicates some kind of doctrinal unwillingness to

render what the text actually suggests – in this case, one assumes, renewed experience of actual childhood. The words translated as 'daily' and 'trespasses' in the Lord's Prayer traditionally cause similar problems, and presumably refer to 'supersubstantiality' and karmic debts respectively.

84   Matt. 24:29, Mk. 13:25, Lk. 21:26: 'The celestial powers will be shaken'. Here, again, the Greek original of the word 'celestial' is *ouranos* – a word which not only has obvious Uranic connections, but also intriguing links with the name of the literally earth-shaking element *uranium*.

85   See, for example, Isa. 24, Joel 2:30–1, Matt. 24:1–30 and the references to a future 'baptism of fire' at Mal. 3:2, 1 Cor. 3:13, Matt, 3:11 and Lk. 3:16 – the 'ordeal' or 'test' of the Lord's Prayer (see note 98).

86   The phrase is used specifically at Matt. 24:8, for example.

87   Matt. 24:37, and compare p. 104.

88   Gen. 8:6–13.

89   Compare Matt. 3:16, Mk. 1:10, Lk. 3:22, Jn. 1:32.

90   Matt. 8:20, Lk. 9:58.

91   Matt. 13:31–2, Mk. 4:30–2, Lk. 13:18–19.

92   Matt. 24:27.

93   Jonah 1–2.

94   Matt: 12:39, 16:4, Lk. 11:29–30.

95   Matt. 16:21, 17:23, 20:19, 27:63, for example – in fulfilment of Hosea 6:2.

96   Rev. 20:4, 2 Pet. 3:8.

97   Matt. 24:31.

98   Compare the Lord's Prayer at Matt. 6:9–13 and Lk. 11:2–4.

99   Matt. 20:17–19, Mk. 11:32–33, Lk. 9:51, 18:31–4.

100   Matt. 21:2–3, Mk. 11:2–3. Lk. 19:30–4.

101   Jesus repeatedly expounds to his disciples the scriptural necessity for his various acts – and notably his martyrdom. See my book *The Armageddon Script* and Schonfield's *The Passover Plot* (Element Books) for a fuller exposition of the notion that Jesus planned his whole mission – including his own death – in deliberate fulfilment of the Messianic prophecies.

102   Zech. 9:9.

103   Compare Isa. 1:3

104   Matt. 21:9.

105   Matt. 21:12, Mk. 11:11.

106   Mk. 11:15, 27.

107   Matt. 24:14.

108   Mk. 13:2.

109   Jn. 2:19.

110   Matt. 9:16–17, Mk. 2:21–2, Lk. 5:36–8.

111   Lk. 22:10–12.

112   Matt. 26:2, Mk. 14:1, 42–3, Lk. 23:54, Jn. 19:31. The chronology
       of the accounts at this point is confused, and Jesus seems to
       have celebrated the Passover some two days early, apparently
       in conformity with the solar calendar of the Essenes. The official,
       lunar Passover appears to have fallen on the sabbath. Cf. Schon-
       field: *The Passover Plot*.

113   In the Genesis creation account, man having been 'made in the
       image of God' on the sixth day, the seventh is the 'day of rest'.

114   Jn. 14:2–3. The Piscean age, as we have already seen, is essentially
       an age for preparation.

115   See Leslie Weatherhead: *The Christian Agnostic* (Hodder & Stough-
       ton, 1965).

116   Jn. 13:2–5.

117   Jn. 13:8.

118   Matt. 26:26–9, Mk. 14:22–4, Lk. 22:17–19. The ritual seems to have
       been identical to the one already long celebrated among the
       Essenes, and similar eucharistic meals – the symbolic eating of
       the god's body and drinking of his blood – are known to have been
       celebrated from antiquity in many of the world's most ancient
       religions.

119   Matt. 26:28, Mk. 14:24, Lk. 22:20. The Damascus Essenes likewise
       referred to themselves as the community of the 'new covenant' or
       'new testament'.

120   Thirteen is immemorially the number of the secret cult-group. The
       origin of the tradition may be purely geometric or Pythagorean,
       since it takes thirteen spheres of equal size to make a symmetrical
       'molecule' of spheres, each in contact with those around it. In this
       case there are twelve 'outer' spheres and one central one, just as the
       twelve disciples 'surround' the central avatar and are thus his link
       with the world. In the Great Pyramid, however, thirteen seems to
       signify 'soul' (Cf. Lemesurier: *The Great Pyramid Decoded*, Element,
       1989).

       Meanwhile the Hebrew for 'one' is *echad*, the numerical value
       of whose letters adds up to thirteen – thus, in the occult tradition,
       confirming the link between thirteen and unity or oneness.

121   Matt. 26:14–16, 27:6–10. The extraordinary episode of Judas Isca-
       riot and the thirty pieces of silver seems to be an allegorical
       reference to the symbolism of the Babylonian zodiac. In ancient
       Babylon (from which, it is well known, many of the oldest Hebrew
       traditions derive) the constellation Aries was replaced by 'The
       Hireling', next to which came 'The Square Field' – i.e. the square
       of Pegasus, a group of stars which overlaps zodiacally both Pisces

and the pot of Aquarius. In fact, then, we could without too much difficulty equate this star-group directly with the 'Potter's Field' mentioned in the gospel account – especially bearing in mind that the gospel's author, like the rest of the Greek-speaking world, would have known Aquarius as 'The Water-Pot' (*Hydrokhoös*). Yet to the Babylonians that same 'Square Field' was seen as representing the Heavenly City itself – here identified, naturally enough, with Babylon rather than its *alter ego*, Jerusalem (compare R. Gleadow: *The Origin of the Zodiac*, Jonathan Cape, 1968). Interpreting the story, then, it would seem that the thirty pieces of silver, by virtue of having paid the wages of the Arian betrayer and so brought about the death of the Piscean avatar, cannot then be paid back into the coffers of the Piscean temple, but must go on to purchase the Heavenly City of Aquarius. In other words, the destruction of the Piscean world by basically Arian hands (compare chapter 4) is seen as an inevitable precondition for the establishment of the Kingdom of Heaven on earth – which the text here seems to describe specifically as 'a burial place for foreigners', in apparent confirmation of other gospel hints that the Kingdom would eventually be taken from Israel and given to the gentile 'dogs', the Messianic Banquet be thrown open to all and sundry.

122 Matt. 17:27.
123 Jn. 3:14.
124 Lk. 23:46.
125 John 19:30.
126 Traditionally the name of the centurion reported by the first three gospels as being on duty at the crucifixion, and whose spear-thrust resulted in the flow of blood and water from the side of the crucified Nazarene (Jn. 19:34). The spear in question seems to have been a source of perennial fascination – not least to Adolf Hitler, who seems to have been convinced that possession of the purported relic must somehow magically confer on him the power of the Aquarian avatarship and the keys of the thousand-year kingdom (Cf. Ravenscroft: *The Spear of Destiny*, Spearman, 1972).
127 The Norse god Odin is said to have hung himself 'for nine days and nine nights on the windy tree' – the world-tree Yggdrasil – and to have pierced his own body with his spear in sacrifice to himself.
128 Matthew 27:51, Mark 15:38, Luke 23:45.
129 Jn. 19:39–42. Whence the significance of the myrrh in the story of the Three Kings.
130 Mk. 4:35–41.
131 Matt. 26:32, Mk. 14:28.
132 John 18:36. Note that 'world' more often than not means 'age' or 'cycle' in the received Christian scriptures. Certainly there is no

sanction in the scriptures for interpreting expressions such as 'the end of the world' in terms of the death of planet Earth or its inhabitants.

133   Matt. 16:28, Mk. 9:1, Lk. 9:27.

134   Ex. 3:7–11.

135   See, for example, Isa. 11:16, Jer. 6:9, 31:7, Joel 2:32. The notion had attained considerable force by the time of Jesus. Amid all the national backsliding and falling by the wayside, it was sufficient for a 'remnant' to remain faithful to re-invoke the ancient covenant between Israel and its god. The idea, as we have seen, was central to the Essene way of life.

136   Matt. 14:22–36.

137   Matthew 28:20.

138   *Vishnu Purana*, describing the present age of Kali.

139   Jn. 21:1–13.

140   Matt. 13:47–50.

141   Matt. 26:29, Mk. 14:25, Lk. 22:18.

142   According to the French Institut Géographique National.

143   The solar bull-cult, of Persian origin – enthusiastically embraced by the Romans – and complete with virgin-birth, cave-nativity on 25th December, and Sunday – the day of the Conquering Sun – as its sacred day.

144   See Rev. 7:14. Christianity's traditional identification of Jesus of Nazareth with the 'Lamb of God' reflects only too aptly its consignment of him to a basically Arian scapegoat-mythology redolent less of the New Covenant than of the Old.

145   Ps. 23, possibly the best-known and least-understood of the psalms.

146   Compare Matt. 7:26–7.

147   Matt. 22:39, Mk. 12:31, Lk. 10:27, Jn. 15:12.

148   One of the constellations of the southern celestial hemisphere, to be found directly to the south of Aquarius. Its chief star is Fomalhaut (from Arabic *Fum al Hút*: 'the fish's mouth'). Traditionally the 'Southern Fish' is shown swallowing the contents of the Aquarian pitcher. Nowadays, its 'mouth' is more usually seen as its 'eye'.

149   See Matt. 10:34.

150   Zech. 4:10.

151   See Matt. 13:24–30.

152   Matt. 25:32–3. Various traditions see sheep and goats as related – even, in the Chinese case, as indistinguishable.

153   Isa. 11:3.

154   Matt. 22:1–14.

155   Matt. 18:13, Lk. 15:7.

156   Matt. 22:11–14.

157 Matt. 13:48. The symbolism is reflected in the Tarot card entitled 'The Star'. (See p. 108).

158 Compare Lk. 16:26.

159 Compare the activities of the first two 'days' of the Genesis creation story.

160 Ps. 23:5.

161 Repeatedly referred to in Matthew – at 8:12, for example.

162 Rev. 21:1.

163 Isa. 2:4, Mic. 4:3–4.

164 See Dr. E.F. Schumacher's stimulating book of the same title. (Blond & Briggs, 1973.)

165 Matt. 4:4, Lk. 4:4.

166 Jn. 6:48–51.

167 Jn. 8:32.

168 Joel 2:28.

169 Mal. 4:2.

170 In the light of the ancient Jewish tradition that the soul of the first *Adam* (= 'man') contained the collective souls of all men, the new being would appear to qualify for the title 'the last Adam' – an expression used by Paul to describe the 'latter Christ' (compare 1 Cor. 15:45–9). Indeed, he seems to describe the New Man specifically at 1 Cor. 12:12–31, and again at Eph. 4:11–16, as a kind of pre-existing spiritual matrix, a heavenly 'head', or mind, into whose body mankind will eventually learn to grow. Meanwhile compare Matt. 18:20, 'Where two or three have met together in my name, I am there among them,' and Gal. 2:20, 'The life I now live is not my life, but the life which Christ lives in me.'

171 Compare the symbolism of the ancient Glastonbury Zodiac.

172 Teilhard de Chardin's term for the goal of man's spiritual evolution seems to be consistent with note 170 above.

173 Matt. 7:7, Lk. 11:9.

174 Suarès, in *The Cipher of Genesis*, sees the Hebrew *mareh* (mirror) as lying at the root of the name 'Mary'. In this case, the latter's scriptural rôle ('Behold the handmaid of the Lord: be it unto me according to thy word') could be of direct significance here.

175 TAT TVAM ASI: 'Thou art that' – one of the basic mottoes of the Vedanta school of philosophy, expressing the identity of the Atman, or soul, with Brahman, the source of all creation.

176 Acts 20:35.

177 Mk. 13:33, Lk. 21:36.

178 Compare the deliberate attempt to develop a 'new age' consciousness and life-style by communities such as the Findhorn Foundation in Moray, Scotland.

179 *Bhagavad Gita* (Tr. J. Mascaró, Penguin, 1972), 10:34. The corresponding card of the Tarot likewise symbolises both deaths and entrances (p.110).

180 Rev. 14:14–16.

181 See Dan. 7:13–14.

182 The fourfold *yoga* (yoke), or path of union, foreshadowed by Jesus of Nazareth, and reflecting in its turn the four independent yogas of Hinduism described in the *Bhagavad Gita* – those of *bhakti, jñana, raja* and *karma* respectively.

183 Compare the symbolism of the Tarot card known as 'The Tower' and the Hindu imagery of Kalki (p.105).

184 Compare the bow-and-arrow symbolism of the Hindus' *Mundaka Upanishad.*

185 Compare Gen. 1:27. The double statement of the text suggests an initial godlike state and a subsequent return to that same situation.

186 Eccl. 12:1–8. Compare the symbolism of 'The Emperor' on p.114

187 1 Corinthians 15:55.

188 Compare Jesus at John 14:2, 'In my Father's house are many mansions.' The Judgement itself is portrayed on page 117.

189 See W. B. Yeats's poem *The Second Coming.*

190 *A Song for St. Cecilia's Day, 1687.*

191 Matt. 2:12.

192 In the Egyptian tradition especially, the soul floats through the underworld on a snake, just as, in the Mayan tradition, Quetzalcoatl is borne away on a raft of snakes towards his destiny. Compare the serpent symbolism of Gemini. The suggestion seems to be that it is ultimately some form of wisdom or knowledge in man that will unlock the door to eternity.

193 Meanwhile, could it be that, in the next 'octave' of cosmic evolution, the zodiacal 'rulers' all move one place to the right (or left), while the signs themselves remain unchanged? Could the zodiacal scheme, in short, have been designed as a kind of computer? If so, then we may have here the basis for a 'cycle of cycles', under the terms of which it would be some 311,000 years before conditions exactly repeated themselves. Such a scheme bears a strong similarity to that propounded by Mme. H. P. Blavatsky in *The Secret Doctrine* (Theosophical University Press, 1888), where she suggests that a period of *seven* such 'cycles of cycles' (or 2,177,000 years) comprises the intended length of the current phase of the human experience, as man gradually experiences all seven 'days' of the creation process – i.e., all seven levels of 'cosmic vibration'. This would date the beginning of that experience geologically to the beginning of the

Pleistocene, a conclusion which correlates interestingly with the findings of palaeontology.

194 From *The Upanishads* (Tr., J. Mascaró. Penguin. 1965).

195 Gen. 8:22.

196 See Gen. 2:16–17, 3:22. The text rightly sees eating from the tree of duality as incompatible with the attainment of the Absolute.

197 A similar pattern may be said to apply to the development of a single human life, if each of the twelve signs be taken to refer to a seven-year phase of personal development.

198 The system adopted by the popular horoscope would have the sun in Aries from March 21st (the spring equinox) until April 19th – an astronomical situation which in fact ceased to apply shortly before the birth of Christ (see diagram p. 2). The actual 'birth-sign' of most present-day people born between those dates is therefore now Pisces, and in the time of our own children and grandchildren it will start to move into Aquarius. In other words, what might be termed 'popular horoscopy' is now almost a whole sign in error, while the constellations themselves are in the wrong 'signs' entirely: most of Aries, for example, is now in the region of the sky known as 'Taurus', while all of Pisces is in 'Aries'.

Curiously enough, this situation reflects exactly the persistent addiction of our present society (theoretically a Piscean one) to anachronistic Arianism (see chapter 4, p. 55). In other words the dichotomy between popular horoscope and stellar reality is perhaps merely a reflection of the current dichotomy between man's consciousness and the greater universe, between Psyche and Cupid – a symptom of, and subconscious symbol for, his own lack of attunement to the cosmos, his unwillingness to move with the times.

Meanwhile it could perhaps be argued that the whole cosmic symphony 'changes key', so to speak, as age succeeds to age, so that each sign in turn takes on the job of the new 'Doh'. Under such terms it could then be argued that the zodiacal signs correspond to a kind of unchanging 'Tonic Sol-Fa' of cosmic relativity, unaffected by the fact that the musical key itself regularly goes up by a further semitone. In which case the birth-sign 'Aries', for example, could be regarded as a kind of psychological constant relative to the 'pitch' of the universe, but having no direct relationship to the actual stars in the sky, which are as it were mute bystanders.

199 In the words of Edgar Cayce, 'Mind is the builder.'

200 Compare Ps.84:10.

201 Ps.90:10.

202 According to Gerald Hawkins (*Beyond Stonehenge*, Hutchinson,

1973), markings on the cave walls of Canchal de Mahoma and Abris de las Viñas (Spain) are astronomical records reflecting a contemporary preoccupation with the moon's phases. They are assigned to the Azilian culture, *which flourished between about 8,000 and 6,000 BC.*